Anonymous

The New Hymn-Book

A collection of hymns for public, social, and domestic worship

Anonymous

The New Hymn-Book
A collection of hymns for public, social, and domestic worship

ISBN/EAN: 9783337290832

Printed in Europe, USA, Canada, Australia, Japan

Cover: Foto ©Thomas Meinert / pixelio.de

More available books at **www.hansebooks.com**

THE NEW HYMN-BOOK.

A COLLECTION

OF

HYMNS

FOR

PUBLIC, SOCIAL, AND DOMESTIC

WORSHIP.

Sing praises to God, sing praises.—PSALM xlvii. 6.
There are no songs comparable to the songs of Zion
MILTON

Nashbille, Tenn.:
SOUTHERN METHODIST PUBLISHING HOUSE.
1881.

.PREFACE.

THE General Conference of the M. E. Church, South, of 1878, adopted the following Resolution:

Resolved, That the Book Agent, with the approval of the Book Editor, the Book Committee, and one of the Bishops, be allowed to publish at pleasure, in the interest of the General Conference, a small hymn or song-book, suited to revival, prayer, and social meetings.

Acting under this authority, the present work has been prepared.

The peculiar taste of no particular person or locality has been consulted in the omissions, abridgments, and additions, but the wants of the entire Connection.

The arrangement in the standard "Hymnbook," and the "Hymn and Tune-book," has been preserved, as well as the most common hymns and tunes in those works, so that it can be used in connection with them.

The compiler of the tunes found it expedient to change the order of some of the hymns in particular sections, in accommodation to the tunes to which they may be sung.

Great care has been taken in the abridgment of hymns, so as not to injure their sentiment or poetical character.

An edition of the hymns without the tunes has been issued for the accommodation of those who may desire it.

The figures in parentheses, at the head of each hymn, refer to the notation in the standard Hymn-book—"Z" refers to "Songs of Zion."

Publishing House of the M. E. Church, South
Nashville, Tennessee, March 16, 1880.

CONTENTS.

(4)

HYMNS.

PART I.
FOR PUBLIC WORSHIP.

SECTION I.
Being and Perfections of God.

1   C. M.   (1)

The Trinity.

A THOUSAND oracles divine
Their common beams unite,
That sinners may with angels join
To worship God aright:

2 To praise a Trinity adored
By all the hosts above;
And one thrice holy God and Lord
Through endless ages love.

3 Triumphant host! they never cease
To laud and magnify
The Triune God of holiness,
Whose glory fills the sky:

4 Whose glory to this earth extends,
When God himself imparts,
And the whole Trinity descends
Into our faithful hearts.

(5)

2   6,6,4,6,6,6,4.   (8)

The Trinity.—Before Sermon.

COME, thou almighty King,
  Help us thy name to sing,
  Help us to praise!
Father all glorious,
O'er all victorious,
Come and reign over us,
  Ancient of days.

2 Come, thou incarnate Word,
Gird on thy mighty sword,
  Our prayer attend:
Come, and thy people bless,
And give thy word success:
Spirit of holiness,
  On us descend!

3 Come, holy Comforter,
Thy sacred witness bear
  In this glad hour:
Thou who almighty art,
Now rule in every heart,
And ne'er from us depart,
  Spirit of power!

4 To the great One and Three
Eternal praises be
  Hence—evermore!
His sovereign majesty
May we in glory see,
And to eternity
  Love and adore.

3   L. M.   (21)

Divine Majesty.

ETERNAL Power, whose high abode
  Becomes the grandeur of a God:
Infinite lengths beyond the bounds
Where stars revolve their little rounds.

2 Thee while the first archangel sings,
He hides his face behind his wings;
And ranks of shining thrones around
Fall worshiping, and spread the ground.

3 Lord, what shall earth and ashes do?
We would adore our Maker too!
From sin and dust to thee we cry,
The Great, the Holy, and the High!

4 Earth from afar hath heard thy fame,
And worms have learned to lisp thy name;
But O! the glories of thy mind
Leave all our soaring thoughts behind!

5 God is in heaven, and men below:
Be short, our tunes; our words, be few!
A solemn reverence checks our songs,
And praise sits silent on our tongues.

4   S. M.   (26)

All-sufficiency.

MY God, my life, my love,
    To thee, to thee I call:
I cannot live if thou remove,
    For thou art all in all.

2 Thy shining grace can cheer
    This dungeon where I dwell:
'T is paradise when thou art here—
    If thou depart, 't is hell.

3 To thee, and thee alone,
    The angels owe their bliss:
They sit around thy gracious throne,
    And dwell where Jesus is.

4 Thou art the sea of love,
    Where all my pleasures roll:
The circle where my passions move,
    And center of my soul.

5 To thee my spirits fly,
   With infinite desire:
And yet how far from thee I lie!
   O Jesus, raise me higher!

5   L. M.   (45)

Opening worship.

O THOU, whom all thy saints adore,
   We now with all thy saints agree,
And bow our inmost souls before
   Thy glorious, awful majesty.

2 We come, great God, to seek thy face,
   And for thy loving-kindness wait;
And O, how dreadful is this place!
   'T is God's own house, 't is heaven's gate.

3 Tremble our hearts to find thee nigh,
   To thee our trembling hearts aspire;
And lo! we see descend from high
   The pillar and the flame of fire.

4 Still let it on th' assembly stay,
   And all the house with glory fill;
To Canaan's bounds point out the way,
   And lead us to thy holy hill.

6   L. M.   (38)

The Father of mercies.

GOD of my life, whose gracious power
   Through various deaths my soul hath led,
Or turned aside the fatal hour,
   Or lifted up my sinking head:

2 In all my ways thy hand I own,
   Thy ruling providence I see:
Assist me still my course to run,
   And still direct my paths to thee.

3 Whither, O whither should I fly,
   But to my loving Saviour's breast?

Secure within thine arms to lie,
  And safe beneath thy wings to rest.

4 I have no skill the snare to shun,
  But thou, O Christ, my wisdom art!
I ever into ruin run,
  But thou art greater than my heart.

5 Foolish, and impotent, and blind,
  Lead me a way I have not known:
Bring me where I my heaven may find,
  The heaven of loving thee alone.

7   C. M.   (29)
          "Doing wonders."

FATHER, how wide thy glory shines!
  How high thy wonders rise!
Known through the earth by thousand signs,
  By thousands through the skies.

2 Those mighty orbs proclaim thy power,
  Their motions speak thy skill;
And on the wings of every hour
  We read thy patience still.

3 But when we view thy strange design
  To save rebellious worms,
Where vengeance and compassion join
  In their divinest forms,

4 Our thoughts are lost in reverent awe;
  We love, and we adore:
The first archangel never saw
  So much of God before.

8   C. M.   (35)
          " Wonderful in counsel."

GOD moves in a mysterious way
  His wonders to perform;
He plants his footsteps in the sea,
  And rides upon the storm.

2 Deep in unfathomable mines
   Of never-failing skill
He treasures up his bright designs,
   And works his sovereign will.

3 Ye fearful saints, fresh courage take:
   The clouds ye so much dread
Are big with mercy, and shall break
   In blessings on your head.

4 Judge not the Lord by feeble sense,
   But trust him for his grace:
Behind a frowning providence
   He hides a smiling face.

5 His purposes will ripen fast,
   Unfolding every hour:
The bud may have a bitter taste,
   But sweet will be the flower.

6 Blind unbelief is sure to err,
   And scan his work in vain:
God is his own interpreter,
   And he will make it plain.

9   C. M.   (37)
Too wise to err—too good to be unkind.

SINCE all the varying scenes of time
   God's watchful eye surveys,
O, who so wise to choose our lot,
   Or to appoint our ways!

2 Good when he gives—supremely good—
   Nor less when he denies:
E'en crosses, from his sovereign hand,
   Are blessings in disguise.

3 Why should we doubt a Father's love,
   So constant and so kind?
To his unerring, gracious will
   Be every wish resigned.

10　　　　L. M.　　　(53)

Psalm c.

BEFORE Jehovah's awful throne,
Ye nations bow with sacred joy:
Know that the Lord is God alone,
He can create, and he destroy.

2 His sovereign power, without our aid,
Made us of clay, and formed us men;
And when, like wandering sheep, we strayed,
He brought us to his fold again.

3 We'll crowd thy gates with thankful songs,
High as the heavens our voices raise;
And earth, with her ten thousand tongues,
Shall fill thy courts with sounding praise.

4 Wide as the world is thy command;
Vast as eternity thy love;
Firm as a rock thy truth must stand,
When rolling years shall cease to move.

11　　　　L. M.　　　(55)

Psalm xxxvi. 5-9.

HIGH in the heavens, eternal God,
Thy goodness in full glory shines;
Thy truth shall break through every cloud
That veils and darkens thy designs.

2 Forever firm thy justice stands,
As mountains their foundations keep;
Wise are the wonders of thy hands,
Thy judgments are a mighty deep.

3 Thy providence is kind and large,
Both man and beast thy bounty share:
The whole creation is thy charge,
But saints are thy peculiar care.

4 My God! how excellent thy grace!
Whence all our hope and comfort springs:
The sons of Adam in distress
Fly to the shadow of thy wings.

5 Life, like a fountain, rich and free,
Springs from the presence of the Lord;
And in thy light our souls shall see
The glories promised in thy word.

12   C. M.   (40)

Exodus xxxiv. 5, 6.

GREAT God! to me the sight afford
To him of old allowed;
And let my faith behold its Lord,
Descending in a cloud!

2 The Lord, the mighty God, thou art,
But let me rather prove
That name inspoken to my heart,
That fav'rite name of Love.

3 Merciful God, thyself proclaim
In this polluted breast:
Mercy is thy distinguished name,
And suits the sinner best.

4 Our mis'ry doth for pity call,
Our sin implores thy grace;
And thou art merciful to all
Our lost, apostate race.

13   C. M.   (41)

Exodus xxxiv. 6, 7.

THY ceaseless, unexhausted love,
Unmerited and free,
Delights our evil to remove,
And help our misery.

2 Thou waitest to be gracious still,
  Thou dost with sinners bear,
That, saved, we may thy goodness feel,
  And all thy grace declare.

3 Thy goodness and thy truth to me,
  To every soul, abound:
A vast unfathomable sea,
  Where all our thoughts are drowned.

4 Its streams the whole creation reach,
  So plenteous is the store;
Enough for all, enough for each,
  Enough forevermore.

14   S. M.   (60)
Psalm ciii. 1–7.

O BLESS the Lord, my soul!
    Let all within me join,
And aid my tongue to bless his name,
  Whose favors are divine.

2 O bless the Lord, my soul!
  Nor let his mercies lie
Forgotten in unthankfulness,
  And without praises die.

3 'T is he forgives thy sins;
  'T is he relieves thy pain;
'T is he who heals thy sicknesses,
  And makes thee young again.

4 He crowns thy life with love,
  When ransomed from the grave:
He, who redeemed my soul from hell,
  Hath sovereign power to save.

15   S. M.   (61)
Psalm ciii. 8–12.

MY soul, repeat His praise,
    Whose mercies are so great;

Whose anger is so slow to rise,
So ready to abate.

2 God will not always chide;
And when his strokes are felt,
His strokes are fewer than our crimes,
And lighter than our guilt.

3 High as the heavens are raised
Above the ground we tread,
So far the riches of his grace
Our highest thoughts exceed.

4 His power subdues our sins;
And his forgiving love,
Far as the east is from the west,
Doth all our guilt remove.

16   S. M.   **(57)**

Psalm xcv.   Opening worship.

COME, sound his praise abroad,
And hymns of glory sing:
Jehovah is the sovereign God,
The universal King.

2 He formed the deeps unknown,
He gave the seas their bound;
The watery worlds are all his own,
And all the solid ground.

3 Come, worship at his throne;
Come, bow before the Lord:
We are his work, and not our own,
He formed us by his word.

4 To-day attend his voice,
Nor dare provoke his rod:
Come, like the people of his choice,
And own your gracious God.

17 S. M. (50)

Psalm xix. *Before morning sermon.*

BEHOLD the morning sun
Begins his glorious way;
His beams through all the nations run,
And life and light convey.

2 But where the gospel comes,
It spreads diviner light;
It calls dead sinners from their tombs,
And gives the blind their sight.

3 How perfect is thy word!
And all thy judgments just:
Forever sure thy promise, Lord,
And men securely trust.

4 My gracious God, how plain
Are thy directions given!
O may I never read in vain,
But find the path to heaven!

18 S. M. (53)

Psalm xxiii.

THE Lord my Shepherd is,
I shall be well supplied:
Since he is mine, and I am his,
What can I want beside?

2 He leads me to the place
Where heavenly pasture grows,
Where living waters gently pass,
And full salvation flows.

3 If e'er I go astray,
He doth my soul reclaim,
And guides me in his own right **way,**
For his most holy name.

4 While he affords his aid,
   I cannot yield to fear:
Though I should walk through death's dark
      shade,
   My Shepherd's with me there.

19   C. M.   (69)

Psalm cxxxix. 1–6.

LORD, all I am is known to thee:
   In vain my soul would try
To shun thy presence, or to flee
   The notice of thine eye.

2 Thy all-surrounding sight surveys
   My rising and my rest,
My public walks, my private ways,
   The secrets of my breast.

3 My thoughts lie open to thee, Lord,
   Before they're formed within;
And ere my lips pronounce the word,
   Thou know'st the sense I mean.

4 O wondrous knowledge! deep and high:
   Where can a creature hide?
Within thy circling arms I lie,
   Beset on every side.

5 So let thy grace surround me still,
   And like a bulwark prove,
To guard my soul from every ill,
   Secured by sovereign love.

20   C. M.   (71)

Psalm cxlv.

LET every tongue thy goodness speak,
   Thou sovereign Lord of all;
Thy strength'ning hands uphold the weak,
   And raise the poor that fall.

2 When sorrows bow the spirit down,
  When virtue lies distressed,
Beneath the proud oppressor's frown,
  Thou giv'st the mourner rest.

3 Thou know'st the pains thy servants feel,
  Thou hear'st thy children's cry;
And their best wishes to fulfill,
  Thy grace is ever nigh.

4 Thy mercy never shall remove
  From men of heart sincere:
Thou sav'st the souls whose humble love
  Is joined with holy fear.

5 My lips shall dwell upon thy praise,
  And spread thy fame abroad:
Let all the sons of Adam raise
  The honors of their God.

21　　　　8, 8, 8.　　　　(72)

Psalm cxlvi.

I'LL praise my Maker while I've breath,
  And when my voice is lost in death,
  Praise shall employ my nobler powers:
My days of praise shall ne'er be past,
While life, and thought, and being last,
  Or immortality endures.

2 Happy the man whose hopes rely
On Israel's God: he made the sky,
  And earth, and seas, with all their train:
His truth forever stands secure:
He saves th' oppressed, he feeds the poor,
  And none shall find his promise vain.

3 The Lord pours eyesight on the blind;
The Lord supports the fainting mind;
  He sends the lab'ring conscience peace;

He helps the stranger in distress,
The widow and the fatherless,
    And grants the prisoner sweet release.

4 I'll praise him while he lends me breath,
And when my voice is lost in death,
    Praise shall employ my nobler powers:
My days of praise shall ne'er be past,
While life, and thought, and being last,
    Or immortality endures.

SECTION II.

Mediation of Christ.

22   7s.   (89)

The Incarnation.

HARK! the herald angels sing,
    "Glory to the new-born King;
Peace on earth, and mercy mild;
God and sinners reconciled:"
Joyful all ye nations rise,
Join the triumphs of the skies;
With th' angelic host proclaim,
"Christ is born in Bethlehem."

2 Christ, by highest heaven adored,
Christ, the everlasting Lord:
Late in time behold him come,
Offspring of a virgin's womb.
Veiled in flesh the Godhead see,
Hail th' incarnate Deity!
Pleased as man with men t' appear,
Jesus our Immanuel here.

3 Hail! the heaven-born Prince of peace!
Hail, the Sun of righteousness!
Light and life to all he brings,
Risen with healing in his wings:
Mild he lays his glory by,
Born that man no more may die;
Born to raise the sons of earth;
Born to give them second birth.

23   C. M.   (99)

Psalm xcviii.

JOY to the world—the Lord is come!
 Let earth receive her King;
Let every heart prepare him room,
 And heaven and nature sing.

2 Joy to the earth—the Saviour reigns!
 Let men their songs employ;
While fields and floods, rocks, hills, and plains,
 Repeat the sounding joy.

3 No more let sins and sorrows grow,
 Nor thorns infest the ground:
He comes to make his blessings flow,
 Far as the curse is found.

4 He rules the world with truth and grace;
 And makes the nations prove
The glories of his righteousness,
 And wonders of his love.

24   C. M.   (88)

The Advent.

HARK! the glad sound! the Saviour comes!
 The Saviour promised long!
Let every heart prepare a throne,
 And every voice a song.

2 He comes the prisoners to release,
  In Satan's bondage held:
The gates of brass before him burst;
  The iron fetters yield!

3 He comes from thickest films of vice
  To clear the mental ray;
And on the eyeballs of the blind
  To pour celestial day.

4 He comes the broken heart to bind,
  The bleeding soul to cure;
And, with the treasures of his grace,
  T' enrich the humble poor.

5 Our glad hosannas, Prince of peace,
  Thy welcome shall proclaim;
And heaven's eternal arches ring
  With thy beloved name.

25   L. M.   (103)
Credentials of Jesus.

BEHOLD the blind their sight receive!
  Behold the dead awake and live!
The dumb speak wonders! and the lame
Leap like the hart, and bless his name!

2 Thus does th' eternal Spirit own,
And seal the mission of the Son;
The Father vindicates his cause,
While he hangs bleeding on the cross.

3 He dies—the heavens in mourning stood!
He rises—and appears a God!
Behold the Lord ascending high,
No more to bleed, no more to die!

4 Hence, and forever, from my heart
I bid my doubts and fears depart;
And to those hands my soul resign,
Which bear credentials so divine.

26 L. M. (105)

His exemplary life.

MY dear Redeemer, and my Lord,
I read my duty in thy word;
But in thy life the law appears,
Drawn out in living characters.

2 Such was thy truth, and such thy zeal,
Such def'rence to thy Father's will,
Such love, and meekness so divine,
I would transcribe, and make them mine.

3 Cold mountains, and the midnight air,
Witnessed the fervor of thy prayer;
The desert thy temptations knew,
Thy conflict, and thy vict'ry too.

- 4 Be thou my pattern: make me bear
More of thy gracious image here;
Then God, the Judge, shall own my name,
Among the followers of the Lamb.

27 7s. (108)

"That ye should follow his steps."

HOLY Lamb, who thee confess,
Followers of thy holiness,
Thee they ever keep in view,
Ever ask, "What shall we do?"
Governed by thy only will,
All thy words we would fulfill,
Would in all thy footsteps go,
Walk as Jesus walked below.

2 While thou didst on earth appear,
Servant to thy servants here,
Mindful of thy place above,
All thy life was prayer and love:
Such our whole employment be,
Works of faith and charity:

Works of love on man bestowed,
Secret intercourse with God.

3 Early in the temple meet,
Let us still our Saviour greet:
Nightly to the mount repair,
Join our praying Pattern there:
There by wrestling faith obtain
Power to work for God again;
Power his image to retrieve,
Power like thee, our Lord, to live.

28   S. M.   (111)

"He beheld the city, and wept over it."

DID Christ o'er sinners weep,
    And shall our cheeks be dry?
Let floods of penitential grief
    Burst forth from every eye.

2 The Son of God in tears
    The wond'ring angels see:
Be thou astonished, O my soul:
    He shed those tears for thee!

3 He wept that we might weep:
    Each sin demands a tear:
In heaven alone no sin is found,
    And there's no weeping there.

29   S. M.   .   (120)

Attraction of the Cross.

BEHOLD th' amazing sight,
    The Saviour lifted high:
Behold the Son of God's delight
    Expire in agony.

2 For whom, for whom, my heart,
    Were all these sorrows borne?

Why did he feel that piercing smart,
And meet that various scorn?

3 For love of us he bled,
And all in torture died;
'T was love that bowed his fainting head,
And oped his gushing side.

4 I see, and I adore
In sympathy of love;
I feel the strong, attractive power
To lift my soul above.

30   C. M.   (123)
The Crucifixion.

BEHOLD the Saviour of mankind
  Nailed to the shameful tree!
How vast the love that him inclined
  To bleed and die for thee!

2 Hark, how he groans! while nature shakes,
  And earth's strong pillars bend!
The temple's vail in sunder breaks,
  The solid marbles rend.

3 'T is done! the precious ransom's paid!
  "Receive my soul!" he cries:
See where he bows his sacred head!
  He bows his head, and dies!

4 But soon he'll break death's envious chain,
  And in full glory shine: ·
O Lamb of God, was ever pain,
  Was ever love, like thine!

31   L. M.   (126)
Gal. vi. 14.

WHEN I survey the wondrous cross
  On which the Prince of glory died,

My richest gain I count but loss,
   And pour contempt on all my pride.

2 Forbid it, Lord, that I should boast,
   Save in the death of Christ, my God;
All the vain things that charm me most,
   I sacrifice them to his blood.

3 See, from his head, his hands, his feet,
   Sorrow and love flow mingled down!
Did e'er such love and sorrow meet?
   Or thorns compose so rich a crown?

4 Were the whole realm of nature mine,
   That were a present far too small;
Love so amazing, so divine,
   Demands my soul, my life, my all.

32   S. M.   (132)

The Fountain.

CALLED from above, I rise,
   And wash away my sin:
The stream to which my spirit flies
   Can make the foulest clean.

2 It runs divinely clear,
   A fountain deep and wide:
'T was opened by the soldier's spear
   In my Redeemer's side!

33   C. M.   (131)

The Fountain.

THERE is a fountain filled with blood,
   Drawn from Immanuel's veins;
And sinners plunged beneath that flood,
   Lose all their guilty stains.

2 The dying thief rejoiced to see
   That fountain in his day;

And there may I, though vile as he,
Wash all my sins away.

3 Dear dying Lamb, thy precious blood
Shall never lose its power,
Till all the ransomed Church of God
Be saved to sin no more.

4 E'er since, by faith, I saw the stream
Thy flowing wounds supply,
Redeeming love has been my theme,
And shall be till I die.

5 Then, in a nobler, sweeter song,
I'll sing thy power to save,
When this poor lisping, stamm'ring tongue
Lies silent in the grave.

34   7,7,7,7,7,7.   (134)

Rock of Ages.

ROCK of ages, cleft for me,
Let me hide myself in thee:
Let the water and the blood,
From thy wounded side which flowed,
Be of sin the double cure,
Save from wrath and make me pure.

2 Could my tears forever flow,
Could my zeal no languor know,
These for sin could not atone;
Thou must save, and thou alone:
In my hand no price I bring,
Simply to thy cross I cling.

3 While I draw this fleeting breath,
When my eyes shall close in death,
When I rise to worlds unknown,
And behold thee on thy throne,
Rock of ages, cleft for me,
Let me hide myself in thee.

35   S. M.   **(135)**

Atoning Sacrifice.

NOT all the blood of beasts,
  On Jewish altars slain,
Could give the guilty conscience peace,
  Or wash away the stain.

2 But Christ, the heavenly Lamb,
  Takes all our sins away;
A sacrifice of nobler name
  And richer blood than they.

3 My faith would lay her hand
  On that dear head of thine—
While like a penitent I stand,
  And there confess my sin.

36   6,6,6,6,8,8.   **(141)**

Resurrection.

YES! the Redeemer rose,
  The Saviour left the dead;
And o'er our hellish foes
  High raised his conqu'ring head:
In wild dismay, The guards around
Fall to the ground, And sink away.

2 Lo! the angelic bands
  In full assembly meet,
To wait his high commands,
  And worship at his feet:
Joyful they come, And wing their way,
From realms of day, To Jesus' tomb.

3 Then back to heaven they fly,
  The joyful news to bear:
Hark! as they soar on high,
  What music fills the air!
Their anthems say, "Jesus, who bled,
Hath left the dead: He rose to-day."

4 Ye mortals, catch the sound,
  Redeemed by Him from hell;
And send the echo round
  The globe on which you dwell;
Transported cry, "Jesus, who bled,
Hath left the dead, No more to die."

5 All hail, triumphant Lord,
  Who sav'st us with thy blood!
Wide be thy name adored,
  Thou rising, reigning God:
With thee we rise, With thee we reign,
And empires gain, Beyond the skies.

37   C. M.   (139)
Resurrection of Christ.

THE Lord of Sabbath let us praise,
  In concert with the blest,
Who, joyful, in harmonious lays
  Employ an endless rest.

2 Thus, Lord, while we remember thee,
  We blest and pious grow;
By hymns of praise we learn to be
  Triumphant here below.

3 On this glad day a brighter scene
  Of glory was displayed,
By God, th' eternal Word, than when
  This universe was made.

4 He rises, who mankind has bought
  With grief and pain extreme:
'T was great to speak the world from naught;
  'T was greater to redeem.

38   S. M.   (142)
Resurrection.

"THE Lord is risen indeed:"
  He lives to die no more:

He lives the sinner's cause to plead,
  Whose curse and shame he bore.
2 "The Lord is risen indeed:"
  Then hell has lost his prey;
With him has risen the ransomed seed,
  To reign in endless day.
3 "The Lord is risen indeed:"
  Attending angels hear—
Up to the courts of heaven, with speed,
  The joyful tidings bear.
4 Then wake your golden lyres,
  And strike each cheerful chord;
Join, all ye bright, celestial choirs,
  To sing our risen Lord.

39   L. M.   (145)
              Dying, rising, reigning.

HE dies! the Friend of sinners dies!
  Lo! Salem's daughters weep around;
A solemn darkness veils the skies;
  A sudden trembling shakes the ground.
Come, saints, and drop a tear or two
  For him who groaned beneath your load:
He shed a thousand drops for you,
  A thousand drops of richer blood.

2 Here's love and grief beyond degree:
  The Lord of glory dies for man!
But lo! what sudden joys we see!
  Jesus, the dead, revives again!
The rising God forsakes the tomb;
  Up to his Father's courts he flies;
Cherubic legions guard him home,
  And shout him welcome to the skies.

3 Break off your tears, ye saints, and tell
  How high your great Deliverer reigns:
Sing how he spoiled the hosts of hell,
  And led the monster death in chains!

Say, "Live forever, wondrous King!
Born to redeem, and strong to save!"
Then ask the monster, "Where's thy sting?"
And, "Where's thy vict'ry, boasting grave?"

40   L. M.   (147)

Psalm xxiv. 7–10.

OUR Lord is risen from the dead;
Our Jesus is gone up on high!
The powers of hell are captive led,
   Dragged to the portals of the sky.
There his triumphal chariot waits,
   And angels chant the solemn lay:
Lift up your heads, ye heavenly gates,
   Ye everlasting doors, give way.

2 Loose all your bars of massy light,
   And wide unfold th' ethereal scene:
He claims these mansions as his right—
   Receive the King of glory in.
Who is the King of glory? Who?
   The Lord that all our foes o'ercame,
The world, sin, death, and hell, o'erthrew—
   And Jesus is the conqu'ror's name.

3 Lo! his triumphal chariot waits,
   And angels chant the solemn lay:
Lift up your heads, ye heavenly gates,
   Ye everlasting doors, give way.
Who is the King of glory? Who?
   The Lord, of glorious power possessed:
The King of saints and angels too,
   God over all forever blessed.

41   7s.   (146)

"Alive forevermore."

CHRIST, the Lord, is risen to-day!
Sons of men and angels say!

Raise your joys and triumphs high:
Sing, ye heavens—thou earth reply.

2 Love's redeeming work is done—
Fought the fight, the battle won:
Lo! the sun's eclipse is o'er;
Lo! he sets in blood no more.

3 Vain the stone, the watch, the seal—
Christ hath burst the gates of hell:
Death in vain forbids his rise:
Christ hath opened paradise.

4 Lives again our glorious King!
"Where, O death! is now thy sting?"
Once he died our souls to save:
"Where's thy victory, boasting grave?"

5 Soar we now where Christ has led,
Following our exalted Head:
Made like him, like him we rise—
Ours the cross, the grave, the skies.

42   7s.   (148)

The Ascension.

HAIL the day that sees him rise,
Ravished from our wishful eyes!
Christ awhile to mortals given,
Reäscends his native heaven.

2 There the pompous triumph waits:
"Lift your heads, eternal gates;
Wide unfold the radiant scene;
Take the King of glory in!"

3 Circled round with angel powers,
Their triumphant Lord, and ours,
Conqueror over death and sin:
Take the King of glory in!

4 Him though highest heaven receives,
Still he loves the earth he leaves:

Though returning to his throne,
Still he calls mankind his own.

5. See, he lifts his hands above!
See, he shows the prints of love!
Hark, his gracious lips bestow
Blessings on his Church below!

6 Ever upward let us move,
Wafted on the wings of love:
Looking when thou, Lord, shalt come,
Longing, gasping after home.

7 There we shall with thee remain,
Partners of thy endless reign:
There thy face unclouded see,
Find our heaven of heavens in thee.

43   8,7.   (154)
Priesthood of Christ.

HAIL, thou once despisèd Jesus!
Hail, thou Galilean King!
Thou didst suffer to release us;
    Thou didst free salvation bring.
Hail, thou agonizing Saviour,
    Bearer of our sin and shame!
By thy merits we find favor;
    Life is given through thy name.

2 Paschal Lamb, by God appointed,
    All our sins on thee were laid;
By almighty love anointed,   .
    Thou hast full atonement made:
All thy people are forgiven,
    Through the virtue of thy blood;
Opened is the gate of heaven;
    Peace is made 'twixt man and God.

3 Jesus, hail! enthroned in glory,
    There forever to abide!

All the heavenly hosts adore thee,
Seated at thy Father's side;
There for sinners thou art pleading, .
There thou dost our place prepare;
Ever for us interceding,
Till in glory we appear.

44   C. M.   (188)
Stupendous Love.

PLUNGED in a gulf of dark despair,
We wretched sinners lay,
Without one cheering beam of hope,
Or spark of glimmering day.

2 With pitying eyes the Prince of grace
Beheld our helpless grief:
He saw, and (O, amazing love!)
He ran to our relief.

3 Down from the shining seats above
With joyful haste he fled,
Entered the grave in mortal flesh,
And dwelt among the dead.

4 O for this love let rocks and hills
Their lasting silence break!
And all harmonious human tongues
The Saviour's praises speak.

5 Angels, assist our mighty joys,
Strike all your harps of gold;
But when you raise your highest notes,
His love can ne'er be told!

45   L. M.   (189)
[From the Latin of St. Bernard.]
Love which passeth knowledge.

OF Him who did salvation bring
I could forever think and sing:

Arise, ye needy, he'll relieve;
Arise, ye guilty, he'll forgive.

2 Ask but his grace, and lo, 't is given!
Ask, and he turns your hell to heaven:
Though sin and sorrow wound my soul,
Jesus, thy balm will make it whole.

3 To shame our sins he blushed in blood,
He closed his eyes to show us God:
Let all the world fall down and know
That none but God such love can show.

4 'T is thee I love, for thee alone
I shed my tears and make my moan!
Where'er I am, where'er I move,
I meet the object of my love.

5 Insatiate to this spring I fly;
I drink, and yet am ever dry:
Ah! who against thy charms is proof?
Ah! who that loves can love enough?

46   L. M.   (193)

Wonders of the Cross.

NATURE with open volume stands
    To spread her Maker's praise abroad;
And every labor of his hands
    Shows something worthy of a God.

2 But in the grace that rescued man
    His brightest form of glory shines:
Here, on the cross, 't is fairest drawn
    In precious blood and crimson lines.

3 O! the sweet wonders of that cross,
    Where God, the Saviour, loved and died!
Her noblest life my spirit draws
    From his dear wounds and bleeding side.

2

4 I would forever speak his name,
  In sound to mortal ears unknown;
With angels join to praise the Lamb,
  And worship at his Father's throne.

47   C. M.   (187)

Indebtedness to Christ.

MAJESTIC sweetness sits enthroned
  Upon the Saviour's brow;
His head with radiant glories crowned,
  His lips with grace o'erflow.

2 He saw me plunged in deep distress,
  And flew to my relief:
For me he bore the shameful cross,
  And carried all my grief.

3 To heaven, the place of his abode,
  He brings my weary feet,
Shows me the glories of my God,
  And makes my joys complete.

4 Since from his bounty I receive
  Such proofs of love divine,
Had I a thousand hearts to give,
  Lord, they should all be thine.

48   C. M.   (153)

Heb. iv. 14–16.

WITH joy we meditate the grace
  Of our High-priest above:
His heart is made of tenderness,
  His bowels melt with love.

2 Touched with a sympathy within,
  He knows our feeble frame:
He knows what sore temptations mean,
  For he hath felt the same.

3 He in the days of feeble flesh
Poured out strong cries and tears;
And in his measure feels afresh
What every member bears.

4 He'll never quench the smoking flax,
But raise it to a flame:
The bruisèd reed he never breaks,
Nor scorns the meanest name.

5 Then let our humble faith address
His mercy and his power:
We shall obtain delivering grace
In the distressing hour.

49   C. M.   (183)
Rev. v. 11–13.

COME, let us join our cheerful songs
With angels round the throne:
Ten thousand thousand are their tongues,
But all their joys are one.

2 Worthy the Lamb that died, they cry,
To be exalted thus:
Worthy the Lamb, our hearts reply,
For he was slain for us.

3 Jesus is worthy to receive
Honor and power divine;
And blessings, more than we can give,
Be, Lord, forever thine.

4 The whole creation join in one
To bless the sacred name
Of him that sits upon the throne,
And to adore the Lamb.

50   C. M.   (196)
The Name of Jesus.

HOW sweet the name of Jesus sounds
In a believer's ear!

It soothes his sorrows, heals his wounds,
And drives away his fear.

2 It makes the wounded spirit whole,
And calms the troubled breast;
'T is manna to the hungry soul,
And to the weary, rest.

3 Weak is the effort of my heart,
And cold my warmest thought·
But when I see thee as thou art,
I 'll praise thee as I ought.

4 Till then, I would thy love proclaim
With every fleeting breath;
And may the music of thy name
Refresh my soul in death!

51   .   C. M.   (197)

"He is precious."

JESUS, I love thy charming name,
'T is music to my ear;
Fain would I sound it out so loud
That earth and heaven should hear.

2 Yes, thou art precious to my soul,
My transport and my trust;
Jewels, to thee, are gaudy toys,
And gold is sordid dust.

3 All my capacious powers can wish,
In thee doth richly meet;
Nor to mine eyes is light so dear,
Nor friendship half so sweet.

4 Thy grace still dwells upon my heart,
And sheds its fragrance there;
The noblest balm of all its wounds,
The cordial of its care.

5 I'll speak the honors of thy name
With my last, laboring breath!
Then speechless clasp thee in mine arms,
The antidote of death.

52   C. M.   (182)

Rev. v. 6–10.

BEHOLD the glories of the Lamb
Amidst his Father's throne!
Prepare new honors for his name,
And songs, before unknown.

2 Let elders worship at his feet,
The Church adore around;
With vials full of odors sweet,
And harps of sweetest sound.

3 Those are the prayers of all the saints,
And these the hymns they raise:
Jesus is kind to our complaints,
He loves to hear our praise.

4 Now to the Lamb that once was slain
Be endless blessings paid:
Salvation, glory, joy, remain,
Forever on thy head.

5 Thou hast redeemed our souls with blood;
Hast set the prisoners free;
Hast made us kings and priests to God;
And we shall reign with thee!

53   C. M.   (160)

"Let all the angels of God worship him."

HOW great the wisdom, power, and grace,
Which in redemption shine!
The heavenly host with joy confess
The work is all divine.

2 Before his feet they cast their crowns—
Those crowns which Jesus gave—

And, with ten thousand thousand tongues,
Proclaim his power to save.

3 They tell the triumphs of his cross,
The sufferings which he bore—
How low he stooped, how high he rose,
And rose to stoop no more.

4 O let them still their voices raise,
And still their songs renew:
Salvation well deserves the praise
Of men and angels too!

54   C. M.   (186)
Salvation.

SALVATION, O the joyful sound!
'T is pleasure to our ears:
A sovereign balm for every wound,
A cordial for our fears.

2 Buried in sorrow and in sin,
At hell's dark door we lay;
But we arise by grace divine
To see a heavenly day.

3 Salvation! let the echo fly
The spacious earth around,
While all the armies of the sky
Conspire to raise the sound.

55   C. M.   (155)
Coronation of Christ.

ALL hail the power of Jesus' name!
Let angels prostrate fall:
Bring forth the royal diadem,
And crown him Lord of all.

2 Ye chosen seed of Israel's race—
A remnant weak and small—
Hail him who saves you by his grace,
And crown him Lord of all.

3 Ye Gentile sinners, ne'er forget
  The wormwood and the gall:
Go, spread your trophies at his feet,
  And crown him Lord of all.

4 Let every kindred, every tribe,
  On this terrestrial ball,
To him all majesty ascribe,
  And crown him Lord of all.

5 O that, with yonder sacred throng,
  We at his feet may fall!
We'll join the everlasting song,
  And crown him Lord of all.

56   S. M.   (194)

Grace.

GRACE! 'tis a charming sound!
  Harmonious to my ear!
Heaven with the echo shall resound,
  And all the earth shall hear.

2 Grace first contrived the way
  To save rebellious man;
And all the steps *that* grace display
  Which drew the wondrous plan.

3 Grace taught my wandering feet
  To tread the heavenly road;
And new supplies each hour I meet
  While pressing on to God.

4 Grace all the work shall crown,
  Through everlasting days:
It lays in heaven the topmost stone,
  And well deserves the praise.

SECTION III.

Offices of the Holy Ghost.

57   L. M.   (205)

Pentecost.

L ORD, we believe to us and ours
  The apostolic promise given:
We wait the pentecostal powers,
  The Holy Ghost sent down from heaven.

2 Ah! leave us not to mourn below,
  Or long for thy return to pine:
Now, Lord, the Comforter bestow,
  And fix in us the Guest Divine.

3 Assembled here with one accord,
  Calmly we wait the promised grace,
The purchase of our dying Lord:
  Come, Holy Ghost, and fill the place.

58   S. M.   (217)

Work and Witness.

O COME, and dwell in me,
  Spirit of power within!
And bring the glorious liberty
  From sorrow, fear, and sin.

2 Hasten the joyful day
  Which shall my sins consume,
When old things shall be done away,
  And all things new become.

3 I want the witness, Lord,
  That all I do is right,

According to thy will and word,
Well-pleasing in thy sight.
4 I ask no higher state;
Indulge me but in this;
And soon or later then translate
To my eternal bliss.

59   S. M.   (206)

Pentecost.

LORD God, the Holy Ghost,
In this accepted hour,
As on the day of Pentecost,
Descend in all thy power!
2 The young, the old, inspire
With wisdom from above;·
And give us hearts and tongues of fire
To pray, and praise, and love.
3 Spirit of light, explore,
And chase our gloom away,
With luster shining more and more
Unto the perfect day.
4 Spirit of truth, be thou
In life and death our guide:
O Spirit of adoption, *now*
May we be sanctified!

60   S. M.   (212)

Spirit of Faith.

SPIRIT of faith, come down,
Reveal the things of God;
And make to us the Godhead known,
And witness with the blood:
'T is thine the blood t' apply,
And give us eyes to see,
Who did for every sinner die,
Hath surely died for me.

2 No man can truly say
  That Jesus is the Lord,
Unless thou take the veil away,
  And breathe the living word:
Then, only then, we feel
  Our interest in his blood,
And cry with joy unspeakable,
  "Thou art my Lord, my God!"

61   L. M.   (224)

His departure earnestly deprecated.

STAY, thou insulted Spirit! stay!
  Though I have done thee such despite;
Nor cast the sinner quite away,
  Nor take thine everlasting flight.

2 Though I have steeled my stubborn heart,
  And still shook off my guilty fears;
And vexed, and urged thee to depart,
  For many long rebellious years:

3 Though I have most unfaithful been
  Of all who e'er thy grace received;
Ten thousand times thy goodness seen,
  Ten thousand times thy goodness grieved;

4 Yet O! the chief of sinners spare,
  In honor of my great High-priest;
Nor in thy righteous anger, swear
  T' exclude me from thy people's rest.

62   S. M.   (220)

His influences sought.

COME, Holy Spirit, come,
  With energy divine,
And on this poor, benighted soul,
  With beams of mercy shine.

2 O melt this frozen heart;
  This stubborn will subdue;
Each evil passion overcome,
  And form me all anew!

3 The profit will be mine,
  But thine shall be the praise;
And unto thee will I devote
  The remnant of my days.

63   C. M.   (213)
Witness and Seal.

WHY should the children of a King
  Go mourning all their days?
Great Comforter, descend, and bring
  The tokens of thy grace.

2 Dost thou not dwell in all thy saints,
  And seal the heirs of heaven?
When wilt thou banish my complaints,
  And show my sins forgiven?

3 Assure my conscience of her part
  In the Redeemer's blood;
And bear thy witness with my heart,
  That I am born of God.

4 Thou art the earnest of his love,
  The pledge of joys to come:
May thy blest wings, celestial Dove,
  Safely convey me home!

64   C. M.   (221)
His quickenings implored.

COME, Holy Spirit, heavenly Dove,
  With all thy quickening powers,
Kindle a flame of sacred love
  In these cold hearts of ours.

2 Look how we grovel here below,
  Fond of these earthly toys;
Our souls how heavily they go
  To reach eternal joys!

3 In vain we tune our formal songs,
  In vain we strive to rise;
Hosannas languish on our tongues,
  And our devotion dies.

4 And shall we then forever live
  At this poor dying rate?
Our love so faint, so cold to thee,
  And thine to us so great?

5 Come, Holy Spirit, heavenly Dove,
  With all thy quickening powers;
Come, shed abroad a Saviour's love,
  And that shall kindle ours.

65   C. M.   (209)

The Interpreter.   Before Sermon.

COME, Holy Ghost, our hearts inspire,
  Let us thine influence prove:
Source of the old prophetic fire,
  Fountain of life and love.

2 Come, Holy Ghost—for, moved by thee,
  The prophets wrote and spoke—
Unlock the truth, thyself the key:
  Unseal the sacred book.

3 Expand thy wings, celestial Dove,
  Brood o'er our nature's night;
On our disordered spirits move,
  And let there now be light.

4 God, through himself, we then shall know,
  If thou within us shine;
And sound, with all thy saints below,
  The depths of love divine.

66   C. M.   (222)

The Spirit invoked.

CELESTIAL Dove, Come from above,
   And guide me in thy ways:
My heart prepare For solemn prayer,
   And tune my lips to praise.

2 Open mine eyes, And make me wise,
   My interest to discern:
From every sin, Without, within,
   Incline my heart to turn.

3 Fly to my aid, When I'm afraid,
   Or plunged in deep distress;
My foes subdue, And bring me through
   This howling wilderness.

SECTION IV.

Institutions of Christianity.

1. THE CHURCH.

67   C. M.   (226)

Psalm xxvii. 1–6.

THE Lord of glory is my light,
   And my salvation too:
God is my strength; nor will I fear
   What all my foes can do.

2 One privilege my heart desires—
   O grant me an abode
Among the Churches of thy saints,
   The temples of my God!

3 There shall I offer my requests,
   And see thy beauty still;

Shall hear thy messages of love,
And there inquire thy will.

4 When troubles rise, and storms appear,
There may his children hide:
God has a strong pavilion, where
He makes my soul abide.

5 Now shall my head be lifted high
Above my foes around;
And songs of joy and victory
Within thy temple sound.

68   L. M.   (227)
Psalm xlvi. 1–5.

GOD is the refuge of his saints,
When storms of sharp distress invade;
Ere we can offer our complaints,
Behold him present with his aid.

2 Let mountains from their seats be hurled
Down to the deep, and buried there—
Convulsions shake the solid world—
Our faith shall never yield to fear.

3 There is a stream, whose gentle flow
Supplies the city of our God;
Life, love, and joy, still gliding through,
And watering our divine abode.

4 That sacred stream, thy holy word,
Our grief allays, our fear controls:
Sweet peace thy promises afford,
And give new strength to fainting souls.

69   L. M.   (233)
Psalm lxxxiv. 1–7.

HOW pleasant, how divinely fair,
O Lord of hosts, thy dwellings are!
With strong desire my spirit faints
To meet th' assemblies of thy saints.

2 Blest are the souls that find a place
Within the temple of thy grace:
Here they behold thy gentler rays,
And seek thy face, and learn thy praise.

3 Blest are the men whose hearts are set
To find the way to Zion's gate:
God is their strength, and through the road
They lean upon their helper, God.

4 Cheerful they walk with growing strength,
Till all shall meet in heaven at length,
Till all before thy face appear,
And join in nobler worship there.

70   C. M.   (238)
Psalm cxxii.

HOW did my heart rejoice to hear
    My friends devoutly say,
"In Zion let us all appear,
    And keep the solemn day!"

2 I love her gates, I love the road!
    The Church, adorned with grace,
Stands like a palace built for God,
    To show his milder face.

3 Peace be within this sacred place,
    And joy a constant guest!
With holy gifts and heavenly grace
    Be her attendants blessed.

4 My soul shall pray for Zion still,
    While life or breath remains;
There my best friends, my kindred dwell,
    There God, my Saviour, reigns.

71   L. M.   (234)
Psalm lxxxiv. 8-12.

GREAT God, attend while Zion sings
    The joy that from thy presence springs:

To spend one day with thee on earth
Exceeds a thousand days of mirth.

2 Might I enjoy the meanest place
Within thy house, O God of grace,
Not tents of ease, nor thrones of power,
Should tempt my feet to leave thy door.

3 God is our sun, he makes our day:
God is our shield, he guards our way
From all th' assaults of hell and sin—
From foes without, and foes within.

4 All needful grace will God bestow,
And crown that grace with glory too:
He gives us all things, and withholds
No real good from upright souls.

72   L. M.   (249)
Isaiah li. 9–11.

A RM of the Lord, awake, awake!
Thine own immortal strength put on!
With terror clothed, hell's kingdom shake,
And cast thy foes with fury down.

2 As in the ancient days, appear;
The sacred annals speak thy fame;
Be now omnipotently near,   .
To endless ages still the same.

3 By death and hell pursued in vain,
To thee the ransomed seed shall come;
Shouting, their heavenly Sion gain,
And pass through death triumphant home.

73   L. M.   (250)
Isaiah lii. 1–12.

A WAKE, Jerusalem, awake!
No longer in thy sins lie down;
The garment of salvation take,
Thy beauty and thy strength put on.

2 Shake off the dust that blinds thy sight,
   And hides the promise from thine eyes;
Arise and struggle into light,
   The great Deliverer calls, Arise!

3 Shake off the bands of sad despair;
   Sion, assert thy liberty;
Look up, thy broken heart prepare,
   And God shall set the captive free.

4 Vessels of mercy, sons of grace,
   Be purged from every sinful stain,
Be like your Lord, his word embrace,
   Nor bear his hallowed name in vain.

5 The Lord shall in your front appear,
   And lead the pompous triumph on;
His glory shall bring up the rear,
   And perfect what his grace begun.

74   S. M.   (245)
          The Church Militant.

JESUS, the Conqueror, reigns,
   In glorious strength arrayed,
His kingdom over all maintains,
   And bids the earth be glad!

2 Ye sons of men rejoice
   In Jesus' mighty love:
Lift up your heart, lift up your voice,
   To Him who rules above.

3 Extol his kingly power;
   Kiss the exalted Son,
Who died, and lives to die no more,
   High on his Father's throne:

4 Our Advocate with God,
   He undertakes our cause,
And spreads through all the earth abroad
   The victory of his cross.

75   S. M.   (247)

The Church Militant.

HARK, how the watchmen cry!
Attend the trumpet's sound!
Stand to your arms, the foe is nigh;
The powers of hell surround.

2 Who bow to Christ's command,
Your arms and hearts prepare;
The day of battle is at hand!
Go forth to glorious war!

3 See, on the mountain top,
The standard of your God!
In Jesus' name I lift it up,
All stained with hallowed blood.

4 His standard-bearer, I
To all the nations call:
Let all to Jesus' cross draw nigh;
He bore the cross for all.

76   L. M.   (237)

Psalm xcii. 12-15.

LORD, 't is a pleasant thing to stand
In gardens planted by thy hand;
Let me within thy courts be seen,
Like a young cedar, fresh and green.

2 There grow thy saints in faith and love,
Blest with thine influence from above:
Not Lebanon, with all its trees,
Yields such a comely sight as these.

3 Laden with fruits of age, they show
The Lord is holy, just, and true:
None that attend his gates shall find
A God unfaithful or unkind.

77 L. M. (243)

Serving the Church.

O MIGHT my lot be cast with these,
  The least of Jesus' witnesses!
O that my Lord would count me meet
To wash his dear disciples' feet!

2 This only thing do I require:
Thou know'st 't is all my heart's desire,
Freely what I receive to give,
The servant of thy Church to live—

3 After my lowly Lord to go,
And wait upon thy saints below;
Enjoy the grace to angels given,
And serve the royal heirs of heaven.

78 8,7. (239)

Supplies of the Church.

GLORIOUS things of thee are spoken,
  Zion, city of our God!
He, whose word can ne'er be broken,
  Formed thee for his own abode:
On the Rock of Ages founded,
  What can shake thy sure repose?
With salvation's walls surrounded,
  Thou may'st smile at all thy foes.

2 See! the streams of living waters,
  Springing from eternal love,
Well supply thy sons and daughters,
  And all fear of want remove:
Who can faint while such a river
  Ever flows, their thirst t' assuage?
Grace which, like the Lord, the giver,
  Never fails from age to age.

3 Round each habitation hovering,
  See the cloud and fire appear,

For a glory and a covering—
Showing that the Lord is near:
Glorious things of thee are spoken,
Zion, city of our God!
He, whose word can ne'er be broken,
Chose thee for his own abode.

2. THE MINISTRY.

79   L. M.   (252)

The Great Commission.

" GO preach my gospel," saith the Lord:
" Bid the whole earth my grace receive;
He shall be saved who trusts my word;
He shall be damned who won't believe.

2 "I'll make your great commission known;
And ye shall prove my gospel true,
By all the works that I have done,
By all the wonders ye shall do.

3 "Teach all the nations my commands;
I'm with you till the world shall end:
All power is trusted in my hands;
I can destroy, and I defend."

4 He spake—and light shone round his head;
On a bright cloud to heaven he rode;
They to the farthest nations spread
The grace of their ascended God.

80   L. M.   (259)

Angels of the Church.

DRAW near, O Son of God, draw near!
Us with thy flaming eye behold;
Still in thy Church vouchsafe t' appear,
And let our candlestick be gold.

2 Still hold the stars in thy right-hand,
And let them in thy luster glow,

The lights of a benighted land,
The angels of thy Church below.

3 Make good their apostolic boast,
Their high commission let them prove,
Be temples of the Holy Ghost,
And filled with faith, and hope, and love.

4 Give them an ear to hear thy word:
Thou speakest to the churches now;
And let all tongues confess their Lord,
Let every knee to Jesus bow.

81   S. M.   (255).

Isaiah lii. 7–10.

HOW beauteous are their feet
Who stand on Zion's hill;
Who bring salvation on their tongues,
And words of peace reveal!

2 How charming is their voice!
How sweet the tidings are!
"Zion, behold thy Saviour King;
He reigns and triumphs here!"

3 How happy are our ears
That hear this joyful sound,
Which kings and prophets waited for,
And sought, but never found!

4 How blessèd are our eyes
That see this heavenly light!
Prophets and kings desired it long,
But died without the sight.

5 The watchmen join their voice,
And tuneful notes employ;
Jerusalem breaks forth in songs,
And deserts learn the joy.

6 The Lord makes bare his arm
Through all the earth abroad:
Let every nation now behold
Their Saviour and their God.

82   C. M.   (258)

Zion's Watchmen.

L ET Zion's watchmen all awake,
  And take th' alarm they give;
Now let them from the mouth of God
Their awful charge receive.

2 'T is not a cause of small import
The pastor's care demands;
But what might fill an angel's heart,
And fill a Saviour's hands.

3 They watch for souls, for which the Lord
Did heavenly bliss forego!
For souls which must forever live
In raptures, or in woe.

4 May they that Jesus whom they preach,
Their own Redeemer see,
And watch thou daily o'er their souls,
That they may watch for thee.

83   S. M.   (271)

For an increase of laborers.

L ORD of the harvest, hear
  Thy needy servant's cry;
Answer our faith's effectual prayer,
And all our wants supply.

2 On thee we humbly wait,
Our wants are in thy view;
The harvest, truly, Lord, is great,
The laborers are few.

3 Convert and send forth more
Into thy Church abroad,
And let them speak thy word of power,
As workers with their God.

4 O let them spread thy name,
Their mission fully prove;
Thy universal grace proclaim,
Thine all-redeeming love.

84   C. M.   (264)

The treasure in earthen vessels.

HOW rich thy bounty, King of kings!
Thy favors, how divine!
The blessings which thy gospel brings,
How splendidly they shine!

2 Gold is but dross, and gems but toys,
Should gold and gems compare;
How mean, when set against those joys,
Thy poorest servants share!

3 Yet all these treasures of thy grace
Are lodged in urns of clay;
And the weak sons of mortal race
Th' immortal gifts convey.

4 Feebly they lisp thy glories forth;
Yet grace the victory gives:
Quickly they molder back to earth;
Yet still thy gospel lives.

5 Such wonders power divine effects;
Such trophies God can raise:
His hand, from crumbling dust, erects
His monuments of praise.

85   C. M.   (265)

The minister's theme.

JESUS, the name high over all
In hell, or earth, or sky!

Angels and men before it fall,
And devils fear and fly.

2 Jesus, the name to sinners dear,
The name to sinners given!
It scatters all their guilty fear:
It turns their hell to heaven.

3 O that the world might taste and see
The riches of his grace!
The arms of love that compass me,
Would all mankind embrace!

4 His only righteousness I show,
His saving truth proclaim:
'T is all my business here below
To cry, "Behold the Lamb!"

5 Happy, if with my latest breath
I may but gasp his name;
Preach him to all, and cry in death,
"Behold, behold the Lamb!"

86   S. M.   (278)

Closing Conference.

AND let our bodies part,
To different climes repair.
Inseparably joined in heart
The friends of Jesus are.

2 The vineyard of the Lord
Before his laborers lies;
And lo! we see the vast reward
Which waits us in the skies.

3 O let our heart and mind
Continually ascend,
That haven of repose to find,
Where all our labors end!

4 Where all our toils are o'er,
   Our suffering and our pain:
Who meet on that eternal shore,
   Shall never part again.

87   S. M.   (272)

Opening Conference.

AND are we yet alive,
   And see each other's face?
Glory and praise to Jesus give
   For his redeeming grace!
Preserved by power divine
   To full salvation here,
Again in Jesus' praise we join,
   And in his sight appear.

2 What troubles have we seen,
   What conflicts have we passed,
Fightings without, and fears within,
   Since we assembled last!
But out of all the Lord
   Hath brought us by his love;
And still he doth his help afford,
   And hides our life above.

3 Then let us make our boast
   Of his redeeming power,
Which saves us to the uttermost,
   Till we can sin no more:
Let us take up the cross,
   Till we the crown obtain;
And gladly reckon all things loss,
   So we may Jesus gain.

88   C. M.   (277)

Closing Conference.

BLEST be the dear uniting love
   That will not let us part:

Our bodies may far off remove,
We still are one in heart.

2 Joined in one spirit to our Head,
Where he appoints we go;
And still in Jesus' footsteps tread,
And show his praise below.

3 Partakers of the Saviour's grace,
The same in mind and heart,
Nor joy, nor grief, nor time, nor place,
Nor life, nor death, can part.

4 But let us hasten to the day
Which shall our flesh restore,
When death shall all be done away,
And bodies part no more.

89   6,6,6,6,8,8.   (276)
Closing Conference.

JESUS, accept the praise
That to thy name belongs!
Matter of all our lays,
Subject of all our songs;
Through thee we now together came,
And part exulting in thy name.

2 In flesh we part awhile,
But still in spirit joined,
T' embrace the happy toil
Thou hast to each assigned;
And while we do thy blessèd will,
We bear our heaven about us still.

3 O let us thus go on
In all thy pleasant ways,
And, armed with patience, run
With joy th' appointed race!
Keep us and every seeking soul,
Till all attain the heavenly goal.

4 There we shall meet again,
When all our toils are o'er,
And death, and grief, and pain,
And parting are no more:
We shall with all our brethren rise,
And grasp thee in the flaming skies.

3. BAPTISM.

90   L. M.   (279)

The commission.—For adults.

'TWAS the commission of our Lord,
  "Go, teach the nations, and baptize:"
The nations have received the word
  Since he ascended to the skies.

2 "Repent, and be baptized," he saith,
  "For the remission of your sins;"
And thus our sense assists our faith,
  And shows us what his gospel means.

3 Our souls he washes in his blood,
  As water makes the body clean;
And the good Spirit from our God
  Descends, like purifying rain.

4 Thus we engage ourselves to thee,
  And seal our covenant with the Lord:
O may the great Eternal Three
  In heaven our solemn vows record!

91   L. M.   (280)

Adult.

COME, Father, Son, and Holy Ghost,
  Honor the means ordained by thee;
Make good our apostolic boast,
  And own thy glorious ministry.

2 We now thy promised presence claim,
  Sent to disciple all mankind—

Sent to baptize into thy name—
We now thy promised presence find.

3 Father, in these reveal thy Son—
In these, for whom we seek thy face,
The hidden mystery make known,
The inward, pure, baptizing grace.

4 Jesus, with us thou always art;
Effectuate now the sacred sign,
The gift unspeakable impart,
And bless the ordinance divine.

5 Eternal Spirit, come from high,
Baptizer of our spirits thou!
The sacramental seal apply,
And witness with the water now.

92   C. M.   (285)
Infant.—Mark x. 13–16.

SEE Israel's gentle Shepherd stand,
With all-engaging charms:
Hark how he calls the tender lambs,
And folds them in his arms!

2 "Permit them to approach," he cries,
"Nor scorn their humble name;
For 't was to bless such souls as these
The Lord of angels came."

3 We bring them, Lord, in thankful hands,
And yield them up to thee;
Joyful that we ourselves are thine,
Thine let our offspring be.

93   C. M.   (286)
Infant.

THUS Lydia sanctified her house,
When she received the word;
Thus the believing jailer gave
His household to the Lord.

2 Thus later saints, eternal King,
  Thine ancient truth embrace:
To thee their infant offspring bring,
  And humbly claim the grace.

94   C. M.   (283)
            Infant.

HOW large the promise, how divine,
  To Abraham and his seed!
"I am a God to thee and thine,
  Supplying all their need."

2 The words of his extensive love
  From age to age endure;
The angel of the covenant proves,
  And seals the blessing sure.

3 Jesus the ancient faith confirms,
  To our great father given;
He takes our children to his arms,
  And calls them heirs of heaven.

4 O God, how faithful are thy ways!
  Thy love endures the same;
Nor from the promise of thy grace
  Blots out our children's name.

4. THE LORD'S SUPPER.

95   C. M.   (288)
            The institution.

THAT doleful night before his death,
  The Lamb for sinners slain
Did, almost with his dying breath,
  This solemn feast ordain.

2 To keep the feast, Lord, we have met,
  And to remember thee:
Help each poor trembler to repeat,
  "For me, he died for me!"

3 Thy sufferings, Lord, each sacred sign
  To our remembrance brings;
We eat the bread, and drink the wine,
  But think on nobler things.

4 O tune our tongues, and set in frame
  Each heart that pants for thee,
To sing "Hosanna to the Lamb!"
  The Lamb that died for me!

96   C. M.   (291)
Remembering Christ.

ACCORDING to thy gracious word,
  In meek humility,
This will I do, my dying Lord,
  I will remember thee.

2 Thy body, broken for my sake,
  My bread from heaven shall be;
Thy testamental cup I take,
  And thus remember thee.

3 Remember thee and all thy pains,
  And all thy love to me;
Yea, while a breath, a pulse remains,
  Will I remember thee.

4 And when these failing lips grow dumb,
  And mind and memory flee,
When thou shalt in thy kingdom come,
  Jesus, remember me.

97   C. M.   (292)
The covenant sealed.

THE promise of my Father's love
  Shall stand forever good:
He said, and gave his soul to death,
  And sealed the grace with blood.

2 To this dear covenant of thy word
  I set my worthless name;

I seal th' engagement to my Lord,
And make my humble claim.
3 Thy light, and strength, and pardoning grace,
And glory, shall be mine;
My life and soul, my heart and flesh,
And all my powers, are thine.
4 Sweet is the memory of his name,
Who blessed us in his will,
And to his testament of love
Made his own blood the seal.

98   L. M.   (294)
              The table prepared.

MY God, and is thy table spread?
And does thy cup with love o'erflow?
Thither be all thy children led,
And let them all its sweetness know.

2 Hail, sacred feast, which Jesus makes!
Rich banquet of his flesh and blood!
Thrice happy he who here partakes
That sacred stream, that heavenly food!

3 O let thy table honored be,
And furnished well with joyful guests!
And may each soul salvation see,
That here its sacred pledges tastes!

4 Let crowds approach with hearts prepared;
With hearts inflamed let all attend;
Nor, when we leave our Father's board,
The pleasure or the profit end.

99   C. M.   (295)
              The invitation.

THE King of heaven his table spreads,
And blessings crown the board;
Not paradise, with all its joys,
Could such delight afford.

2 Pardon and peace to dying men,
And endless life, are given,
Through the rich blood that Jesus shed,
To raise our souls to heaven.

3 Millions of souls, in glory now,
Were fed and feasted here;
And millions more, still on the way,
Around the board appear.

4 All things are ready: come away,
Nor weak excuses frame;
Crowd to your places at the feast,
And bless the Founder's name.

100   C. M.   (296)
Penitent sinners' welcome.

THIS is the feast of heavenly wine,
And God invites to sup;
The juices of the living Vine
Were pressed to fill the cup.

2 O bless the Saviour, ye who eat,
With royal dainties fed;
Not heaven affords a costlier treat,
For Jesus is the bread!

3 The vile, the lost—he calls to them:
"Ye trembling souls, appear!
The righteous in their own esteem
Have no acceptance here.

4 "Approach, ye poor, nor dare refuse
The banquet spread for you:"
Dear Saviour, this is welcome news!
Then I may venture too.

101   S. M.   (297)
"Let us keep the feast."

LET all who truly bear
The bleeding Saviour's name,

Their faithful hearts with us prepare,
And eat the paschal Lamb.

2 Who thus our faith employ
His sufferings to record,
E'en now we mournfully enjoy
Communion with our Lord;

3 As though we every one
Beneath his cross had stood,
And seen him heave, and heard him groan,
And felt his gushing blood.

4 We too with him are dead,
And shall with him arise:
The cross on which he bows his head
Shall lift us to the skies.

O2   L. M.   (303)

The penitent at the table.

HOW long, thou faithful God, shall I
Here in thy ways forgotten lie?
When shall the means of healing be
The channels of thy grace to me?

2 Sinners, on every side, step in,
And wash away their pain and sin;
But I, a helpless, sin-sick soul,
Still lie expiring at the pool.

3 In vain I take the broken bread,
I cannot on thy mercy feed;
In vain I drink the hallowed wine,
I cannot taste the love divine.

4 Surely if thou the symbols bless,
The covenant-blood shall seal my peace;
Thy flesh, e'en now, shall be my food,
And all my soul be filled with God.

3

5. THE SABBATH.

103   7,7,7,7,7,7.   (315)

Opening morning service.

SAFELY through another week
God has brought us on our way;
Let us now a blessing seek,   .
Waiting in his courts to-day:
Day of all the week the best,
Emblem of eternal rest.

2 While we seek supplies of grace,
Through the dear Redeemer's name,
Show thy reconciling face—
Take away our sin and shame:
From our worldly cares set free,
May we rest this day in thee.

3 Here we come thy name to praise;
Let us feel thy presence near;
May thy glory meet our eyes,
While we in thy house appear:
Here afford us, Lord, a taste
Of our everlasting feast.   .

4 May the gospel's joyful sound
Conquer sinners, comfort saints,
Make the fruits of grace abound,
Bring relief from all complaints:
Thus let all our Sabbaths prove,
Till we join the Church above.

104   C. M.   •   (314)

Opening morning service.

COME, let us join with one accord
In hymns around the throne!
This is the day our rising Lord
Hath made and called his own.

2 This is the day which God hath blessed,
  The brightest of the seven,
Type of that everlasting rest
  The saints enjoy in heaven.

3 Then let us in his name sing on,
  And hasten to that day
When our Redeemer shall come down,
  And shadows pass away.

4 Not one, but all our days below,
  Let us in hymns employ;
And in our Lord rejoicing, go
  To his eternal joy.

105   L. M.   (316)
Opening morning service.

ANOTHER six days' work is done;
  Another Sabbath is begun:
Return, my soul, enjoy thy rest,
Improve the day thy God hath blessed.

2 O that our thoughts and thanks may rise,
As grateful incense, to the skies;
And draw from Christ that sweet repose
Which none but he that feels it knows!

3 This heavenly calm within the breast
Is the dear pledge of glorious rest,
Which for the Church of God remains,
The end of cares, the end of pains.

4 In holy duties let the day,
In holy comforts, pass away:
How sweet, a Sabbath thus to spend,
In hope of one that ne'er shall end!

106   L. M.   (320)
Psalm xcii.

SWEET is the work, my God, my King,
  To praise thy name, give thanks, and sing;

To show thy love by morning light,
And talk of all thy truth by night.

2 Sweet is the day of sacred rest;
No mortal cares shall seize my breast:
O may my heart in tune be found,
Like David's harp of solemn sound!

3 My heart shall triumph in my Lord,
And bless his works and bless his word:
Thy works of grace, how bright they shine!
How deep thy counsels! how divine!

4 Then shall I share a glorious part
When grace hath well refined my heart,
And fresh supplies of joy are shed,
Like holy oil, to cheer my head.

5 Then shall I see, and hear, and know,
All I desired or wished below;
And every power find sweet employ
In that eternal world of joy.

107   L. M.   (323)

In the sanctuary.

FAR from my thoughts, vain world, begone!
Let my religious hours alone:
Fain would my eyes my Saviour see;
I wait a visit, Lord, from thee.

2 My heart grows warm with holy fire,
And kindles with a pure desire:
Come, my dear Jesus, from above,
And feed my soul with heavenly love.

3 Blest Jesus, what delicious fare!
How sweet thine entertainments are!
Never did angels taste above
Redeeming grace and dying love.

108   L. M.   (324)

The eternal Sabbath.

THINE earthly Sabbaths, Lord, we love;
But there's a nobler rest above;
To that our laboring souls aspire,
With ardent pangs of strong desire.

2 No more fatigue, no more distress;
Nor sin nor hell shall reach the place;
No sighs shall mingle with the songs
Which warble from immortal tongues.

3 No rude alarms of raging foes;
No cares to break the long repose;
No midnight shade, no clouded sun,
But sacred, high, eternal noon.

4 O long-expected day, begin;
Dawn on these realms of woe and sin:
Fain would we leave this weary road,
And sleep in death, to rest with God.

SECTION V.

The Gospel Call.

109   6,6,6,6,8,8.   (325)

The year of Jubilee.

BLOW ye the trumpet, blow,
The gladly solemn sound;
Let all the nations know,
To earth's remotest bound,
The year of jubilee is come;
Return, ye ransomed sinners, home.

2 Extol the Lamb of God,
The all-atoning Lamb;
Redemption through his blood
Throughout the world proclaim:

The year of jubilee is come;
Return, ye ransomed sinners, home.

3 Ye slaves of sin and hell,
   Your liberty receive,
And safe in Jesus dwell,
   And blest in Jesus live:
The year of jubilee is come;
Return, ye ransomed sinners, home.

4 Ye who have sold for naught
   Your heritage above,
Receive it back unbought,
   The gift of Jesus' love:
The year of jubilee is come;
Return, ye ransomed sinners, home.

5 The gospel trumpet hear,
   The news of heavenly grace;
And, saved from earth, appear
   Before your Saviour's face:
The year of jubilee is come;
Return, ye ransomed sinners, home.

110   L. M.   (328)

The hearty welcome.

COME, sinners, to the gospel feast;
   Let every soul be Jesus' guest:
Ye need not one be left behind,
For God hath bidden all mankind.

2 Come, all ye souls by sin oppressed,
Ye restless wanderers after rest,
Ye poor, and maimed, and halt, and blind,
In Christ a hearty welcome find.

3 See him set forth before your eyes,
That precious, bleeding sacrifice!
His offered benefits embrace,
And freely now be saved by grace!

111 L. M. (331)

Isaiah lv. 1-3.

HO! every one that thirsts, draw nigh;
'T is God invites the fallen race:
Mercy and free salvation buy;
    Buy wine, and milk, and gospel grace.

2 Come to the living waters, come!
Sinners, obey your Maker's call:
Return, ye weary wanderers, home,
    And find my grace is free for all.

3 See from the rock a fountain rise;
For you in healing streams it rolls;
Money ye need not bring, nor price,
    Ye laboring, burdened, sin-sick souls.

4 Nothing ye in exchange shall give;
Leave all you have, and are, behind;
Frankly the gift of God receive,
    Pardon and peace in Jesus find.

112 L. M. (354)

"Now is the accepted time."

WHILE life prolongs its precious light,
Mercy is found, and peace is given;
But soon, ah soon, approaching night
    Shall blot out every hope of heaven.

2 While God invites, how blest the day!
How sweet the gospel's charming sound!
Come, sinners, haste, O haste away,
    While yet a pardoning God is found.

3 Soon, borne on time's most rapid wing,
Shall death command you to the grave,
Before his bar your spirits bring,
    And none be found to hear or save. .

4 In that lone land of deep despair
  No Sabbath's heavenly light shall rise,
No God regard your bitter prayer,
  No Saviour call you to the skies.

113   L. M.   (351)

"Return unto me."

RETURN, O wanderer, return!
  And seek an injured Father's face;
Those warm desires that in thee burn
  Were kindled by reclaiming grace.

2 Return, O wanderer, return,
  And seek a Father's melting heart;
His pitying eyes thy grief discern,
  His hand shall heal thine inward smart.

3 Return, O wanderer, return,
  Thy Saviour bids thy spirit live;
Go to his bleeding feet, and learn
  How freely Jesus can forgive.

4 Return, O wanderer, return,
  And wipe away the falling tear;
'Tis God who says, "No longer mourn;"
  'Tis mercy's voice invites thee near.

114   L. M.   (326)

The gospel supper.

SINNERS, obey the gospel word!
  Haste to the supper of my Lord:
Be wise to know your gracious day;
  All things are ready; come away.

2 Ready the Father is to own
  And kiss his late-returning son:
Ready your loving Saviour stands,
  And spreads for you his bleeding hands.

3 Ready the Spirit of his love
Just now your hardness to remove;
T' apply and witness with the blood,
And wash and seal the sons of God.

4 Ready for you the angels wait,
To triumph in your blest estate:
Tuning their harps, they long to praise
The wonders of redeeming grace.

5 The Father, Son, and Holy Ghost,
Are ready with their shining host:
All heaven is ready to resound,
"The dead's alive! the lost is found!"

115   C. M.   (334)
Come to Jesus.

COME, humble sinner, in whose breast
   A thousand thoughts revolve—
Come, with your guilt and fear oppressed
And make this last resolve:

2 I'll go to Jesus, though my sin
Hath like a mountain rose;
I know his courts, I'll enter in,
Whatever may oppose:

3 Prostrate I'll lie before his throne,
And there my guilt confess;
I'll tell him I'm a wretch undone,
Without his sovereign grace:

4 I'll to the gracious King approach,
Whose scepter pardon gives;
Perhaps he may command my touch,
And then the suppliant lives.

5 Perhaps he may admit my plea,
Perhaps will hear my prayer;
But if I perish, I will pray,
And perish only there.

6 I can but perish if I go,
   I am resolved to try;
For if I stay away, I know
   I must forever die.

7 But if I die with mercy sought,
   When I the King have tried,
This were to die (delightful thought!)
   As sinner never died.

116   C. M.   · (353)
            Urgent appeal.

SINNERS, the voice of God regard:
   'T is mercy speaks to-day;
He calls you by his sacred word
   From sin's destructive way.

2 Like the rough sea that cannot rest,
   You live devoid of peace;
A thousand stings within your breast
   Deprive your souls of ease.

3 Your way is dark, and leads to hell:
   Why will you persevere?
Can you in endless torments dwell,
   Shut up in black despair?

4 Why will you in the crooked ways
   Of sin and folly go?
In pain you travel all your days,
   To reap eternal woe.

5 But he that turns to God shall live
   Through his abounding grace:
His mercy will the guilt forgive
   Of those that seek his face.

117   C. M.   (350)
         Revelation iii. 20.

COME, let us who in Christ believe,
   Our common Saviour praise:

To him, with joyful voices, give
The glory of his grace.

2 He now stands knocking at the door
Of every sinner's heart:
The worst need keep him out no more,
Or force him to depart.

3 Through grace we hearken to thy voice,
Yield to be saved from sin;
In sure and certain hope rejoice,
That thou wilt enter in.

4 Come quickly in, thou heavenly Guest,
Nor ever hence remove;
But sup with us, and let the feast
Be everlasting love.

118   C. M.   (357)
Acts xvii. 30, 31.

REPENT, the voice celestial cries,
No longer dare delay;
The wretch that scorns the mandate dies,
And meets a fiery day.

2 The summons goes through all the earth,
Let earth attend and fear:
Listen, ye men of royal birth,
And let your vassals hear.

3 Together in his presence bow,
And all your guilt confess;
Accept the offered Saviour now,
Nor trifle with the grace.

4 Bow, ere the awful trumpet sound,
And call you to his bar;
For mercy knows th' appointed bound,
And turns to vengeance there.

119   C. M.   (333)

Isaiah lv. 1–3.

LET every mortal ear attend,
   And every heart rejoice;
The trumpet of the gospel sounds
   With an inviting voice.

2 Ho! all ye hungry, starving souls,
   That feed upon the wind,
And vainly strive with earthly toys
   To fill an empty mind—

3 Eternal wisdom hath prepared
   A soul-reviving feast,
And bids your longing appetites
   The rich provision taste.

4 Ho! ye that pant for living streams,
   And pine away and die,
Here you may quench your raging thirst
   With springs that never dry.

5 Rivers of love and mercy here
   In a rich ocean join:
Salvation, in abundance, flows
   Like floods of milk and wine.

6 The happy gates of gospel grace
   Stand open night and day:
Lord, we are come to seek supplies,
   And drive our wants away.

120   C. M.   (368)

Before an awakening sermon.

COME, O thou all-victorious Lord,
   Thy power to us make known;
Strike with the hammer of thy word,
   And break these hearts of stone.

2 Convince us first of unbelief,
   And freely then release:

Fill every soul with sacred grief,
And then with sacred peace.

3 Impoverish, Lord, and then relieve,
And then enrich the poor:
The knowledge of our sickness give,
The knowledge of our cure.

4 That blessed sense of guilt impart,
And then remove the load:
Trouble, and wash the troubled heart
In the atoning blood.

5 Our desperate state through sin declare,
And speak our sins forgiven:
By perfect holiness prepare,
And take us up to heaven.

121   7s.   (345)

The expostulation.

SINNERS, turn, why will ye die?
God, your Maker, asks you why—
God, who did your being give,
Made you with himself to live:
He the fatal cause demands,
Asks the work of his own hands,
Why, ye thankless creatures, why
Will ye cross his love, and die?

2 Sinners, turn, why will ye die?
God, your Saviour, asks you why—
God, who did your souls retrieve,
Died himself that ye might live:
Will ye let him die in vain?
Crucify your Lord again?
Why, ye ransomed sinners, why
Will ye slight his grace, and die?

3 Sinners, turn, why will ye die?
God, the Spirit, asks you why—

He, who all your lives hath strove,
Wooed you to embrace his love:
Will ye not his grace receive?
Will ye still refuse to live?
Why, ye long-sought sinners, why
Will ye grieve your God, and die?

122   7s.   (360)
"Escape for thy life."

HASTEN, sinner, to be wise;
   Stay not for the morrow's sun;
Wisdom, if thou still despise,
Harder is she to be won.

2 Hasten, mercy to implore;
   Stay not for the morrow's sun;
Lest thy season should be o'er
Ere this evening's stage be run.

3 Hasten, sinner, to return;
   Stay not for the morrow's sun;
Lest thy lamp should cease to burn
Ere salvation's work is done.

4 Hasten, sinner, to be blest;
   Stay not for the morrow's sun;
Lest the curse should thee arrest
Ere the morrow is begun.

123   C. M.   (371)
Before an inviting sermon.

JESUS, thou all-redeeming Lord,
   Thy blessing we implore;
Open the door to preach thy word,
The great effectual door.

2 Gather the outcasts in, and save
   From sin and Satan's power;
And let them now acceptance have,   ,
   And know their gracious hour.

3 Lover of souls! thou know'st to prize
  What thou hast bought so dear:
Come, then, and in thy people's eyes,
  With all thy wounds appear!

4 Ready thou art the blood t' apply,
  And prove the record true;
And all thy wounds to sinners cry,
  "I suffered this for you!"

124   C. M.   (341)

The free invitation.

JESUS, thy blessings are not few,
  Nor is thy gospel weak:
Thy grace can melt the stubborn Jew,
  And bow th' aspiring Greek.

2 Wide as the reach of Satan's rage
  Doth thy salvation flow;
'T is not confined to sex or age,
  The lofty or the low.

3 While grace is offered to the prince,
  The poor may take their share;
No mortal has a just pretense
  To perish in despair.

4 Come, all ye vilest sinners, come;
  He 'll form your souls anew:
His gospel and his heart have room
  For rebels such as you.

125   C. M.   (366)

Before evening sermon.

THOU Son of God, whose flaming eyes
  Our inmost thoughts perceive,
Accept the evening sacrifice
  Which now to thee we give.

2 We bow before thy gracious throne,
And think ourselves sincere;
But show us, Lord, is every one
Thy real worshiper?

3 Is here a soul that knows thee not,
Nor feels his want of thee;
A stranger to the blood which bought
His pardon on the tree?

4 Convince him now of unbelief,
His desperate state explain;
And fill his heart with sacred grief,
And penitential pain.

5 Speak with that voice that wakes the dead,
And bid the sleeper rise;
And bid his guilty conscience dread
The death that never dies.

126   C. M.   (365)
Eccles. xii. 1.

IN the soft season of thy youth,
In nature's smiling bloom,
Ere age arrives, and trembling waits
Its summons to the tomb,
Remember thy Creator now;
For him thy powers employ;
Make him thy fear, thy love, thy hope,
Thy confidence and joy.

2 He shall defend and guide thy youth
Through life's uncertain sea,
Till thou art landed on the coast
Of blest eternity.
Then seek the Lord betimes, and choose
The path of heavenly truth:
This earth affords no lovelier sight
Than a religious youth.

127   S. M.   (355)

"Now is the day of salvation."

TO-MORROW, Lord, is thine,
    Lodged in thy sovereign hand,
And if its sun arise and shine,
    It shines by thy command.

2 The present moment flies,
    And bears our life away;
O make thy servants truly wise,
    That they may live to-day!

3 One thing demands our care;
    O be it still pursued,
Lest, slighted once, the season fair
    Should never be renewed!

4 To Jesus may we fly,
    Swift as the morning light,
Lest life's young golden beam should die
    In sudden, endless night.

128   L. M.   (349)

Revelation iii. 20.

BEHOLD a Stranger at the door!
    He gently knocks, has knocked before;
Has waited long—is waiting still;
You treat no other friend so ill.

2 O lovely attitude! He stands
With melting heart and bleeding hands;
O matchless kindness! and he shows
This matchless kindness to his foes!

3 But will he prove a Friend indeed?
He will; the very Friend you need;
The Friend of sinners—yes, 't is He,
With garments dyed on Calvary.

4 Rise, touched with gratitude divine;
Turn out his enemy and thine,
That soul-destroying monster, sin,
And let the heavenly Stranger in.

5 Admit him, ere his anger burn;
His feet departed, ne'er return;
Admit him, or the hour's at hand,
You'll at his door rejected stand.

129   8,7,8,7,4,7.   (330)

The invitation.

COME, ye sinners, poor and needy,
  Weak and wounded, sick and sore;
Jesus ready stands to save you,
    Full of pity, love, and power:
          He is able,
    He is willing: doubt no more.

2 Now, ye needy, come and welcome,
    God's free bounty glorify:
True belief and true repentance,
    Every grace that brings you nigh,
          Without money,
    Come to Jesus Christ and buy.

3 Let not conscience make you linger;
    Nor of fitness fondly dream;
All the fitness he requireth
    Is to feel your need of him:
          This he gives you,
    'T is the Spirit's glimmering beam.

4 Come, ye weary, heavy-laden,
    Bruised and mangled by the fall,
If you tarry till you're better,
    You will never come at all:
          Not the righteous,
    Sinners Jesus came to call.

130   11,10,11,10.   (352)

Come, ye disconsolate.

COME, ye disconsolate, where'er ye languish,
Come, and at God's altar fervently kneel;
Here bring your wounded hearts, here tell your
    anguish;
Earth has no sorrow that Heaven cannot heal.

2 Joy of the desolate, Light of the straying,
Hope of the penitent, fadeless and pure,
Here speaks the Comforter, in God's name say-
    ing,
Earth has no sorrow that Heaven cannot cure.

3 Go, ask the infidel what boon he brings us—
What charm for aching hearts *he* can reveal,
Sweet as the heavenly promise hope sings us,
Earth has no sorrow that God cannot heal.

SECTION VI.

Penitential Exercises.

131   7,6,7,6,7,8,7,6.   (379)

Praying for repentance.

JESUS, let thy pitying eye
Call back a wandering sheep;
False to thee, like Peter, I
Would fain like Peter, weep.
Let me be by grace restored;
On me be all long-suffering shown:
Turn, and look upon me, Lord,
And break my heart of stone.

2 Saviour, Prince, enthroned above,
Repentance to impart,
Give me, through thy dying love,
The humble, contrite heart:

Give what I have long implored,
  A portion of thy grief unknown:
Turn, and look upon me, Lord,
  And break my heart of stone.

3 Look as when thy languid eye
  Was closed that we might live:
"Father" (at the point to die
  My Saviour gasped), "forgive!"
Surely with that dying word
  He turns, and looks, and cries, "'T is done!"
O my bleeding, loving Lord,
  Thou break'st my heart of stone!

132   L. M.   (380)
        Psalm li. 1–4.

SHOW pity, Lord, O Lord, forgive,
  Let a repenting rebel live:
Are not thy mercies large and free?
May not a sinner trust in thee?

2 My crimes are great, but do n't surpass
The power and glory of thy grace:
Great God, thy nature hath no bound,
So let thy pardoning love be found.

3 O wash my soul from every sin!
And make my guilty conscience clean!
Here on my heart the burden lies,
And past offenses pain mine eyes.

4 My lips with shame my sins confess,
Against thy law, against thy grace:
Lord, should thy judgments grow severe,
I am condemned, but thou art clear.

5 Yet save a trembling sinner, Lord,
Whose hope, still hovering round thy word,
Would light on some sweet promise there,
Some sure support against despair.

33 L. M. (381)

Psalm li. 5–8.

LORD, we are vile, conceived in sin.
And born unholy and unclean;
Sprung from the man whose guilty fall
Corrupts his race, and taints us all.

2 Soon as we draw our infant breath,
The seeds of sin grow up for death:
Thy law demands a perfect heart,
But we're defiled in every part.

3 Behold, I fall before thy face;
My only refuge is thy grace:
No outward forms can make me clean;
The leprosy lies deep within.

4 Jesus, my God, thy blood alone
Hath power sufficient to atone;
Thy blood can make me white as snow:
No Jewish types could cleanse me so.

5 While guilt disturbs and breaks my peace,
Nor flesh nor soul hath rest or ease:
Lord, let me hear thy pardoning voice,
And make my broken heart rejoice.

34 S. M. (375)

Praying for repentance.

O THAT I could repent,
With all my idols part;
And to thy gracious eye present
A humble, contrite heart:

2 A heart with grief oppressed
For having grieved my God;
A troubled heart that cannot rest
Till sprinkled with thy blood.

3 Jesus, on me bestow
  The penitent desire;
With true sincerity of woe
  My aching breast inspire:

4 With softening pity look,
  And melt my hardness down:
Strike with thy love's resistless stroke,
  And break this heart of stone!

135   C. M.   (377)

Praying for repentance.

O FOR that tenderness of heart,
  Which bows before the Lord,
Acknowledging how just thou art,
  And trembling at thy word!
O for those humble, contrite tears,
  Which from repentance flow;
That consciousness of guilt which fears
  The long suspended blow!

2 Saviour, to me in pity give
  The sensible distress;
The pledge thou wilt, at last, receive,
  And bid me die in peace:
Wilt from the dreadful day remove,
  Before the evil come;
My spirit hide with saints above
  My body in the tomb.

136   S. M.   (394)

Surrendering the heart.

WHEN shall thy love constrain
  And force me to thy breast?
When shall my soul return again
  To her eternal rest?

2 Ah! what avails my strife,
  My wandering to and fro?

Thou hast the words of endless life:
Ah! whither should I go?

3 Thy condescending grace
To me did freely move:
It calls me still to seek thy face,
And stoops to ask my love.

4 Lord, at thy feet I fall,
I groan to be set free:
I fain would now obey the call,
And give up all for thee.

C. M.   (421)

"Help thou my unbelief."

HOW sad our state by nature is!
Our sin how deep it stains!
And Satan binds our captive souls
Fast in his slavish chains.

2 But there's a voice of sovereign grace
Sounds from the sacred word:
Ho! ye despairing sinners, come,
And trust a faithful Lord.

3 My soul obeys the gracious call,
And runs to this relief:
I would believe thy promise, Lord,
O help my unbelief!

4 To the blest fountain of thy blood,
Incarnate God, I fly:
Here let me wash my spotted soul
From crimes of deepest dye.

5 A guilty, weak, and helpless worm,
Into thy arms I fall:
Be thou my strength and righteousness,
My Jesus and my all.

138   7s.   (433)

Refuge in Christ.

JESUS, Lover of my soul,
    Let me to thy bosom fly,
While the nearer waters roll,
    While the tempest still is high:
Hide me, O my Saviour, hide,
    Till the storm of life be past;
Safe into the haven guide,
    O receive my soul at last!

2 Other refuge have I none,
    Hangs my helpless soul on thee:
Leave, ah! leave me not alone,
    Still support and comfort me!
All my trust on thee is stayed,
    All my help from thee I bring:
Cover my defenseless head
    With the shadow of thy wing.

3 Thou, O Christ, art all I want;
    More than all in thee I find:
Raise the fallen, cheer the faint,
    Heal the sick, and lead the blind.
Just and holy is thy name;
    I am all unrighteousness:
False, and full of sin, I am;
    Thou art full of truth and grace.

4 Plenteous grace with thee is found,
    Grace to cover all my sin:
Let the healing streams abound,
    Make and keep me pure within:
Thou of life the fountain art;
    Freely let me take of thee:
Spring thou up within my heart,
    Rise to all eternity!

139   C. M.   (435)

Subdued by the Cross.

IN evil long I took delight,
  Unawed by shame or fear;
Till a new object struck my sight,
  And stopped my wild career.

2 I saw one hanging on a tree,
  In agonies and blood,
Who fixed his languid eyes on me,
  As near his cross I stood.

3 Sure, never to my latest breath
  Can I forget that look;
It seemed to charge me with his death,
  Though not a word he spoke.

4 My conscience felt, and owned the guilt,
* And plunged me in despair:
I saw my sins his blood had spilt,
  And helped to nail him there.

5 A second look he gave, which said,
  "I freely all forgive;
This blood is for thy ransom paid;
  I died that thou may'st live."

6 Thus, while his death my sin displays
  In all its blackest hue,
Such is the mystery of grace,
  It seals my pardon too.

140   C. M.   (424)

Praying for faith.

FATHER, I stretch my hands to thee,
  No other help I know;
If thou withdraw thyself from me,
  Ah! whither shall I go?

2 What did thine only Son endure,
    Before I drew my breath!
What pain, what labor to secure
    My soul from endless death!

3 Author of faith, to thee I lift
    My weary, longing eyes:
O let me now receive that gift!
    My soul without it dies!

4 Surely thou canst not let me die:
    O speak, and I shall live;
And here I will unwearied lie,
    Till thou thy Spirit give.

5 The worst of sinners would rejoice,
    Could they but see thy face:
O let me hear thy quickening voice,
    And taste thy pardoning grace!

141   C. M.   **(449)**

The backslider's prayer.

O FOR a closer walk with God,
    A calm and heavenly frame,
A light to shine upon the road
    That leads me to the Lamb!

2 Where is the blessedness I knew
    When first I saw the Lord?
Where is the soul-refreshing view
    Of Jesus and his word?

3 What peaceful hours I once enjoyed!
    How sweet their memory still!
But they have left an aching void
    The world can never fill.

4 Return, O holy Dove, return,
    Sweet messenger of rest!
I hate the sins that made thee mourn,
    And drove thee from my breast.

5 The dearest idol I have known,
  Whate'er that idol be,
Help me to tear it from thy throne,
  And worship only thee.
6 So shall my walk be close with God,
  Calm and serene my frame;
So purer light shall mark the road
  That leads me to the Lamb.

1-1-2   S. M.   (395)
Surrendering the heart.

A ND can I yet delay
   My little all to give?
To tear my soul from earth away
  For Jesus to receive?
2 Nay, but I yield, I yield!
  I can hold out no more:
I sink, by dying love compelled,
  And own thee conqueror!
3 Though late, I all forsake;
  My friends, my all resign:
Gracious Redeemer, take, O take,
  And seal me ever thine!
4 Come, and possess me whole,
  Nor hence again remove:
Settle and fix my wavering soul
  With all thy weight of love.

143   S. M.   (410)
Embracing offered mercy.

O MY offended God,
   If now at last I see
That I have trampled on thy blood,
  And done despite to thee:
2 If I begin to wake
  Out of my deadly sleep

Into thy arms of mercy take,
And there forever keep.

3 No other right have I
Than what the world may claim:
All, all may to their God draw nigh,
Through faith in Jesus' name.

4 Thou hast obtained the grace
That all may turn and live;
And lo! thy offer I embrace,
Thy mercy I receive.

144   7s.   (87 Z.)
The suit.

COME, my soul, thy suit prepare—
Jesus loves to answer prayer:
He himself has bid thee pray,
Therefore will not say thee nay.

2 Thou art coming to the King:
Large petitions with thee bring;
For his grace and power are such,
None can ever ask too much.

3 With my burden I begin:
Lord, remove this load of sin!
Let thy blood, for sinners spilt,
Set my conscience free from guilt.

4 Lord, I come to thee for rest—
Take possession of my breast:
There thy blood-bought right maintain,
And without a rival reign.

145   L. M.   (414)
"Heal my soul."

O THOU, whom once they flocked to hear!
Thy words to hear, thy power to feel;
Suffer the sinners to draw near,
And graciously receive us still.

2 They that be whole, thyself hast said,
 No need of a physician have;
But I am sick, and want thine aid,
 And ask thine utmost power to save.

3 Thy power, and truth, and love divine,
 The same from age to age endure:
A word, a gracious word of thine,
 The most inveterate plague can cure.

4 Helpless howe'er my spirit lies,
 And long hath languished at the pool,
A word of thine shall make it rise,
 Shall speak me in a moment whole.

146   C. M.   (425)
 Surrendering at the cross.

ALAS! and did my Saviour bleed?
 And did my Sovereign die?
Would he devote that sacred head
 For such a worm as I?

2 Was it for crimes that I had done
 He groaned upon the tree?
Amazing pity! grace unknown!
 And love beyond degree!

3 Well might the sun in darkness hide,
 And shut his glories in,
When Christ, the mighty Maker, died
 For man, the creature's, sin!

4 Thus might I hide my blushing face,
 While his dear cross appears;
Dissolve my heart in thankfulness,
 And melt mine eyes to tears.

5 But drops of grief can ne'er repay
 The debt of love I owe:
Here, Lord, I give myself away,
 'T is all that I can do.

147   C. M.   (427)
The effort.

APPROACH, my soul, the mercy-seat,
  Where Jesus answers prayer;
There humbly fall before his feet,
  For none can perish there.

2 Thy promise is my only plea,
  With this I venture nigh:
Thou call'st the burdened soul to thee,
  And such, O Lord, am I.

3 Bowed down beneath a load of sin,
  By Satan sorely pressed,
By wars without, and fears within,
  I come to thee for rest.

4 Be thou my shield and hiding-place,
  That, sheltered near thy side,
I may my fierce accuser face,
  And tell him thou hast died.

5 O wondrous love, to bleed and die,
  To bear the cross and shame,
That guilty sinners, such as I,
  Might plead his gracious name!

6 "Poor tempest-tossèd soul, be still,
  My promised grace receive:"
'T is Jesus speaks—I must, I will,
  I can, I do believe.

148   L. M.   (428)
"I am the way."

JESUS, my all, to heaven is gone,
  He whom I fix my hopes upon;
His track I see, and I'll pursue
The narrow way, till him I view.

2 The way the holy prophets went,
The road that leads from banishment,

The King's highway of holiness,
I'll go, for all his paths are peace.

3 This is the way I long have sought,
And mourned because I found it not:
My grief a burden long has been,
Because I was not saved from sin.

4 The more I strove against its power,
I felt its weight and guilt the more;
Till late I heard my Saviour say,
"Come hither, soul, I AM THE WAY."

5 Lo! glad I come, and thou, blest Lamb
Shalt take me to thee as I am;
Nothing but sin have I to give,
Nothing but love shall I receive.

6 Then will I tell to sinners round
What a dear Saviour I have found;
I'll point to thy redeeming blood,
And say, "Behold the way to God!"   .

149   8,8,6.   (436)
Panting for the love of God.

O LOVE divine, how sweet thou art!
When shall I find my willing heart
All taken up by thee?
I thirst, I faint, I die to prove
The greatness of redeeming love,
The love of Christ to me.

2 Stronger his love than death or hell;
Its riches are unsearchable:
The first-born sons of light
Desire in vain its depths to see;
They cannot reach the mystery,
The length, the breadth, and height.

3 God only knows the love of God:
O that it now were shed abroad
In this poor stony heart!

For love I sigh, for love I pine:
This only portion, Lord, be mine!
   Be mine this better part!
4 O that I could forever sit
With Mary at the Master's feet!
   Be this my happy choice:
My only care, delight, and bliss,
My joy, my heaven on earth, be this,
   To hear the Bridegroom's voice!

150   8,8,8,8,8,8.   (441)
        Wrestling Jacob.

COME, O thou Traveler unknown,
   Whom still I hold, but cannot see;
My company before is gone,
   And I am left alone with thee:
With thee all night I mean to stay,
And wrestle till the break of day.

2 I need not tell thee who I am;
   My sin and misery declare:
Thyself hast called me by my name,
   Look on thy hands and read it there;
But who, I ask thee, who art thou?
Tell me thy name, and tell me now.

3 In vain thou strugglest to get free;
   I never will unloose my hold!
Art thou the Man that died for me?
   The secret of thy love unfold:
Wrestling, I will not let thee go,
Till I thy name, thy nature know.

4 Wilt thou not yet to me reveal
   Thy new, unutterable name?
Tell me, I still beseech thee, tell;
   To know it now, resolved I am:
Wrestling, I will not let thee go,
Till I thy name, thy nature know.

151   8,8,8,8,8,8.   (442)

Concluded.

YIELD to me now, for I am weak,
  But confident in self-despair:
Speak to my heart, in blessings speak;
  Be conquered by my instant prayer:
Speak, or thou never hence shalt move,
And tell me if thy name is Love.

2 'Tis Love! 'Tis Love! thou diedst for me;
  I hear thy whisper in my heart:
The morning breaks, the shadows flee;
  Pure, universal love thou art:
To me, to all, thy bowels move,
Thy nature and thy name is Love.

3 I know thee, Saviour, who thou art,
  Jesus, the feeble sinner's Friend;
Nor wilt thou with the night depart,
  But stay and love me to the end:
Thy mercies never shall remove:
Thy nature and thy name is Love.

4 Lame as I am, I take the prey;
  Hell, earth, and sin, with ease o'ercome;
I leap for joy, pursue my way,
  And, as a bounding hart, fly home;
Through all eternity to prove
Thy nature and thy name is Love.

152   7s.   (453)

The backslider's plea.

DEPTH of mercy! can there be
  Mercy still reserved for me?
Can my God his wrath forbear?
Me, the chief of sinners, spare?

2 I have long withstood his grace,
Long provoked him to his face;

4

Would not hearken to his calls;
Grieved him by a thousand falls.

3 Lo! I cumber still the ground:
Lo! an Advocate is found!
"Hasten not to cut him down:
Let this barren soul alone."

4 Jesus speaks, and pleads his blood:
He disarms the wrath of God!
Now my Father's bowels move;
Justice lingers into love.

5 Kindled his relentings are;
Me he now delights to spare;
Cries, "How shall I give thee up?"
Lets the lifted thunder drop.

6 There for me the Saviour stands;
Shows his wounds and spreads his hands:
God is love! I know, I feel;
Jesus weeps and loves me still.

153   8,8,8,6.   (104 Z.)

The venture.

JUST as I am—without one plea,
But that thy blood was shed for me,
And that thou bidst me come to thee—
   O Lamb of God, I come!

2 Just as I am—and waiting not
To rid my soul of one dark blot,
To thee, whose blood can cleanse each spot,
   O Lamb of God, I come!

3 Just as I am—though tossed about
With many a conflict, many a doubt,
With fears within and wars without—
   O Lamb of God, I come!

4 Just as I am—poor, wretched, blind:
' Sight, riches, healing of the mind,
Yea, all I need, in thee to find,
   O Lamb of God, I come!

5 Just as I am—thy love unknown
Has broken every barrier down:
Now to be thine, yea, thine alone,
   O Lamb of God, I come!

SECTION VII.

Christian Experience.

1. JUSTIFICATION AND THE NEW BIRTH.

154   C. M.   (456)
Opening worship.

O FOR a thousand tongues to sing
  My great Redeemer's praise!
The glories of my God and King,
  The triumphs of his grace!

2 My gracious Master and my God,
  Assist me to proclaim,
To spread through all the earth abroad
  The honors of thy Name.

3 Jesus! the Name that charms our fears,
  That bids our sorrows cease;
'Tis music in the sinner's ears,
  'Tis life, and health, and peace.

4 He breaks the power of canceled sin,
  He sets the prisoner free:
His blood can make the foulest clean;
  His blood availed for *me*.

5 He speaks—and, listening to his voice,
  New life the dead receive;

The mournful, broken hearts rejoice; .
The humble poor believe.

6 Hear him, ye deaf; his praise, ye dumb,
Your loosened tongues employ;
Ye blind, behold your Saviour come,
And leap, ye lame, for joy.

155   C. M.   (476)
"The fruit of the Spirit is—joy."

JOY is a fruit that will not grow
In nature's barren soil:
All we can boast, till Christ we know,
Is vanity and toil.

2 But where the Lord has planted grace,
And made his glories known,
There fruits of heavenly joy and peace
Are found—and there alone.

3 A bleeding Saviour seen by faith,
A sense of pardoning love,
A hope that triumphs over death,
Give joys like those above.

4 To take a glimpse within the vail,
To know that God is mine,
Are springs of joy that never fail,
Unspeakable, divine!

5 These are the joys which satisfy,
And sanctify, the mind;
Which make the spirit mount on high,
And leave the world behind.

156   6,6,6,6,8,8.   (469)
"Whereby we cry, Abba, Father."

ARISE, my soul, arise,
Shake off thy guilty fears,
The bleeding Sacrifice
In my behalf appears:

Before the throne my Surety stands,
My name is written on his hands.

2 He ever lives above,
   For me to intercede;
His all-redeeming love,
   His precious blood, to plead:
His blood atoned for all our race,
And sprinkles now the throne of grace.

3 Five bleeding wounds he bears,
   Received on Calvary:
They pour effectual prayers,
   They strongly speak for me:
"Forgive him, O forgive," they cry,
"Nor let that ransomed sinner die!"

4 The Father hears him pray,
   His dear Anointed One:
He cannot turn away
   The presence of his Son:
His Spirit answers to the blood,
And tells me I am born of God.

5 My God is reconciled,
   His pardoning voice I hear:
He owns me for his child,
   I can no longer fear:
With confidence I now draw nigh,
And Father, Abba, Father, cry.

157   6,6,6,6,8,8.   (177)

The Saviour's praise.

LET earth and heaven agree,
   Angels and men be joined,
To celebrate with me
   The Saviour of mankind;
T' adore the all-atoning Lamb,
And bless the sound of Jesus' name.

2 Stung by the scorpion, sin,
    My poor expiring soul
The balmy sound drinks in,
    And is at once made whole:
See there my Lord upon the tree!
I hear, I feel he died for me.

3 O unexampled love!
    O all-redeeming grace!
How swiftly didst thou move
    To save a fallen race!
What shall I do to make it known
What thou for all mankind hast done?

4 O for a trumpet voice,
    On all the world to call!
To bid their hearts rejoice
    In him who died for all!
For all my Lord was crucified;
For all, for all my Saviour died.

158   L. M.   (480)

Proverbs iii. 13–18.

HAPPY the man that finds the grace,
    The blessing of God's chosen race,
The wisdom coming from above,
The faith that sweetly works by love.

2 Happy beyond description, he
Who knows "the Saviour died for me!"
The gift unspeakable obtains,
And heavenly understanding gains.

3 Wisdom divine! who tells the price
Of wisdom's costly merchandise?
Wisdom to silver we prefer,
And gold is dross compared to her.

4 Her hands are filled with length of days,
True riches and immortal praise—

Riches of Christ on all bestowed,
And honor that descends from God.

5 To purest joys she all invites,
Chaste, holy, spiritual delights:
Her ways are ways of pleasantness,
And all her flowery paths are peace.

6 Happy the man who wisdom gains;
Thrice happy who his guest retains:
He owns, and shall forever own,
' Wisdom, and Christ, and heaven, are one.

159   C. M.   (481)

God the source of joy.

MY God, the spring of all my joys,
The life of my delights,
The glory of my brightest days,
And comfort of my nights!

2 In darkest shades if thou appear,
My dawning is begun;
Thou art my soul's bright morning star,
And thou my rising sun.

3 The opening heavens around me shine
With beams of sacred bliss,
If Jesus show his mercy mine,
And whisper I am his.

4 My soul would leave this heavy clay,
At that transporting word,
Run up with joy the shining way,
To see and praise my Lord.

5 Fearless of hell and ghastly death,
I'd break through every foe;
The wings of love and arms of faith
Would bear me conqueror through.

160   L. M.   (458)

Opening worship.

JESUS, thou everlasting King,
Accept the tribute which we bring:
Accept thy well-deserved renown,
And wear our praises as thy crown.

2 Let every act of worship be
Like our espousals, Lord, to thee—
Like the blest hour, when from above
We first received the pledge of love.

3 The gladness of that happy day,
O may it ever, ever stay!
Nor let our faith forsake its hold,
Nor hope decline, nor love grow cold!

4 Each following minute, as it flies,
Increase thy praise, improve our joys,
Till we are raised to sing thy name
At the great supper of the Lamb.

161   L. M.   (460)

[From the German of Zinzendorf.]

Receiving the atonement.

JESUS, thy blood and righteousness
My beauty are, my glorious dress:
Midst flaming worlds, in these arrayed,
With joy shall I lift up my head.

2 Bold shall I stand in thy great day,
For who aught to my charge shall lay?
Fully absolved through these I am,
From sin and fear, from guilt and shame.

3 The holy, meek, unspotted Lamb,
Who from the Father's bosom came,
Who died for me, e'en me t' atone,
Now for my Lord and God I own.

4 Lord, I believe thy precious blood,
Which, at the mercy-seat of God,

Forever doth for sinners plead,
For *me*, e'en for *my* soul, was shed.

5 Lord, I believe were sinners more
Than sands upon the ocean shore,
Thou hast for ALL a ransom paid,
For ALL a full atonement made.

162   L. M.   (461)
The work of faith.

AUTHOR of faith, eternal Word,
  Whose Spirit breathes the active flame,
Faith, like its Finisher and Lord,
  To-day, as yesterday, the same:

2 To thee our humble hearts aspire,
  And ask the gift unspeakable:
Increase in us the kindled fire,
  In us the work of faith fulfill.

3 To him that in thy name believes,
  Eternal life with thee is given:
Into himself he all receives—
  Pardon, and holiness, and heaven.

4 Faith lends its realizing light,
  The clouds disperse, the shadows fly,
Th' Invisible appears in sight,
  And God is seen by mortal eye.

163   S. M.   (466)
Witness of adoption.

HOW can a sinner know
  His sins on earth forgiven?
How can my gracious Saviour show
  My name inscribed in heaven!

2 What we have felt and seen,
  With confidence we tell;
And publish to the sons of men
  The signs infallible.

3 We who in Christ believe
That he for us hath died,
We all his unknown peace receive,
And feel his blood applied.

4 Exults our rising soul,
Disburdened of her load,
And swells unutterably full
Of glory and of God.

164   S. M.   (465)
Adoption.

BEHOLD! what wondrous grace
The Father hath bestowed
On sinners of a mortal race—
To call them sons of God!

2 Nor does it yet appear
How great we must be made;
But when we see our Saviour here,
We shall be like our Head.

3 A hope so much divine
May trials well endure,
May purge our souls from sense and sin,
As Christ, the Lord, is pure.

4 If in my Father's love
I share a filial part,
Send down thy Spirit, like a dove,
To rest upon my heart.

5 We would no longer lie
Like slaves beneath the throne,
My faith shall Abba, Father, cry,
And thou the kindred own.

165   8,7,8,7,4,7.   (471)
"Whom not having seen, we love."

O THOU God of my salvation,
My Redeemer from all sin,

Moved by thy divine compassion,
  Who hast died my heart to win,
    I will praise thee:
  Where shall I thy praise begin?

2 Though unseen, I love the Saviour:
  He hath brought salvation near—
Manifests his pardoning favor,
  And, when Jesus doth appear,
    Soul and body
  Shall his glorious image bear.

3 While the angel choirs are crying,
  Glory to the great I AM!
I with them will still be vying,
  Glory! glory to the Lamb!
    O how precious
  Is the sound of Jesus' name!

4 Angels now are hovering round us,
  Unperceived they mix the throng,
Wondering at the love that crowned us,
  Glad to join the holy song:
    Hallelujah!
Love and praise to Christ belong!

1 66   7s.   (473)
Love to the Saviour.

HARK, my soul, it is the Lord!
  'T is thy Saviour, hear his word!
Jesus speaks, he speaks to thee:
  "Say, poor sinner, lov'st thou me?

2 "I delivered thee when bound,
And, when bleeding, healed thy wound;
Sought thee wandering, set thee right,
Turned thy darkness into light.

3 "Can a mother's tender care
Cease toward the child she bare?
Yes, she may forgetful be,
Yet will I remember thee

4 "Mine is an unchanging love,
Higher than the heights above,
Deeper than the depths beneath,
Free and faithful, strong as death.
5 "Thou shalt see my glory soon,
When the work of faith is done;
Partner of my throne shalt be:
Say, poor sinner, lov'st thou me?"
6 Lord, it is my chief complaint
That my love is still so faint;
Yet I love thee and adore:
O for grace to love thee more!

167   L. M.   (488)
"Our rejoicing is this"—

LORD, how secure and blest are they
Who feel the joys of pardoned sin!
Should storms of wrath shake earth and sea,
Their minds have heaven and peace within.
2 The day glides sweetly o'er their heads,
Made up of innocence and love;
And soft and silent as the shades
Their nightly minutes gently move.
3 Quick as their thoughts their joys come on,
But fly not half so fast away:
Their souls are ever bright as noon,
And calm as summer evenings be.
4 How oft they look to th' heavenly hills,
Where groves of living pleasures grow!
And longing hopes and cheerful smiles
Sit undisturbed upon their brow.

168   L. M.   (477)
[From the German.]
Love and joy.

I THIRST, thou wounded Lamb of God,
To wash me in thy cleansing blood;

To dwell within thy wounds: then pain
Is sweet, and life or death is gain.

2 Take my poor heart, and let it be
Forever closed to all but thee!
Seal thou my breast, and let me wear
That pledge of love forever there.

3 How blest are they who still abide
Close sheltered in thy bleeding side!
Who life and strength from thence derive,
And by thee move, and in thee live.

4 What are our works but sin and death,
Till thou thy quickening Spirit breathe?
Thou giv'st the power thy grace to move:
O wondrous grace! O boundless love!

169   L. M.   (478)

Concluded.

HOW can it be, thou heavenly King,
That thou shouldst us to glory bring?
Make slaves the partners of thy throne,
Decked with a never-fading crown!

2 Hence our hearts melt, our eyes o'erflow,
Our words are lost, nor will we know,
Nor will we think, of aught beside,
"My Lord, my Love is crucified."

3 Ah! Lord, enlarge our scanty thought,
To know the wonders thou hast wrought:
Unloose our stammering tongues to tell
Thy love immense, unsearchable.

4 First-born of many brethren thou,
To thee, lo, all our souls we bow:
To thee our hearts and hands we give;
Thine may we die, thine may we live.

170   11,9.   (483)
Ecstasy of the new-born soul.

HOW happy are they Who their Saviour obey,
And have laid up their treasures above!
Tongue cannot express The sweet comfort and
  peace
Of a soul in its earliest love!

2 That comfort was mine, When the favor divine
I first found in the blood of the Lamb:
When my heart it believed, What a joy I re-
  ceived,
What a heaven in Jesus's name!

3 'T was a heaven below My Redeemer to know,
And the angels could do nothing more
Than fall at his feet, And the story repeat,
And the Lover of sinners adore.

4 Jesus all the day long Was my joy and my
  song:
O that all his salvation might see!
He hath loved me, I cried, He hath suffered
  and died,
To redeem a poor rebel like me.

5 On the wings of his love I was carried above
All sin, and temptation, and pain:
I could not believe That I ever should grieve,
That I ever should suffer again.

6 O the rapturous height Of that holy delight
Which I felt in the life-giving blood!
Of my Saviour possessed, I was perfectly blessed,
As if filled with the fullness of God.

171   6,6,4,6,6,6,4.   (103 Z.)
Self-consecration at the cross.

MY faith looks up to thee,
Thou Lamb of Calvary,
  Saviour divine!

Now hear me while I pray:
Take all my guilt away:
O let me from this day
    Be wholly thine.

2 May thy rich grace impart
Strength to my fainting heart,
    My zeal inspire:
As thou hast died for me,
O may my love to thee,
Pure, warm, and changeless be—
    A living fire.

3 While life's dark maze I tread,
And griefs around me spread,
    Be thou my guide:
Bid darkness turn to day,
Wipe sorrow's tears away,
Nor let me ever stray
    From thee aside!

4 When ends life's transient dream,
When death's cold, sullen stream
    Shall o'er me roll—
Blest Saviour, then in love
Fear and distrust remove:
O bear me safe above—
    A ransomed soul!

172   8,7.   (479)
Sitting at the Cross.

SWEET the moments, rich in blessing,
  Which before the cross I spend;
Life, and health, and peace possessing,
  From the sinner's dying Friend:
Here it is I find my heaven,
  While upon the Lamb I gaze:
Love I much? I've much forgiven—
  I'm a miracle of grace!

2 Love and grief my heart dividing,
  With my tears his feet I 'll bathe;
Constant still in faith abiding,
  Life deriving from his death.
May I still enjoy this feeling,
  In all need to Jesus go;
Prove his wounds each day more healing,
  And himself more deeply know.

2. ENTIRE SANCTIFICATION AND PERFECT
LOVE.

173   C. M.   (494)
Perfect purification.

FOREVER here my rest shall be,
  Close to thy bleeding side;
This all my hope, and all my plea,
  For me the Saviour died.

2 My dying Saviour, and my God,
  Fountain for guilt and sin,
Sprinkle me ever with thy blood,
  And cleanse and keep me clean.

3 Wash me, and make me thus thine own;
  Wash me, and mine thou art;
Wash me, but not my feet alone,
  My hands, my head, my heart.

4 Th' atonement of thy blood apply,
  Till faith to sight improve,
Till hope in full fruition die,.
  And all my soul be love.

174   C. M.   (497)
The rest of faith.

LORD, I believe a rest remains,
  To all thy people known;
A rest where pure enjoyment reigns,
  And thou art loved alone:

2 A rest where all our soul's desire
  Is fixed on things above;
Where fear, and sin, and grief, expire,
  Cast out by perfect love.

3 O that I now the rest might know,
  Believe, and enter in!
Now, Saviour, now the power bestow,
  And let me cease from sin!

4 Remove this hardness from my heart,
  This unbelief remove:
To me the rest of faith impart,
  The Sabbath of thy love.

175   L. M.   (533)

Seeking perfect rest in Christ.

O THAT my load of sin were gone!
    O that I could at last submit
At Jesus' feet to lay it down!
  To lay my soul at Jesus' feet!

2 Rest for my soul I long to find:
  Saviour of all, if mine thou art,
Give me thy meek and lowly mind,
  And stamp thine image on my heart.

3 Break off the yoke of inbred sin,
  And fully set my spirit free:
I cannot rest till pure within,
  Till I am wholly lost in thee.

4 Fain would I learn of thee, my God;
  Thy light and easy burden prove,
The cross, all stained with hallowed blood,
  The labor of thy dying love.

5 I would, but thou must give the power;
  My heart from every sin release;
Bring near, bring near the joyful hour,
  And fill me with thy perfect peace.

176   L. M.   (526)

[From the French.]

The act of consecration.

COME, Saviour, Jesus, from above!
  Assist me with thy heavenly grace;
Empty my heart of earthly love,
  And for thyself prepare the place.

2 O let thy sacred presence fill,
  And set my longing spirit free,
Which pants to have no other will,
  But day and night to feast on thee.

3 While in this region here below,
  No other good will I pursue:
I'll bid this world of noise and show,
  With all its glittering snares, adieu!

4 That path with humble speed I'll seek,
  In which my Saviour's footsteps shine,
Nor will I hear, nor will I speak,
  Of any other love but thine.

5 Henceforth may no profane delight
  Divide this consecrated soul;
Possess it, thou, who hast the right,
  As Lord and Master of the whole.

177   C. M.   (504)

Longing to be established in love.

COME, Lord, and claim me for thine own:
  Saviour, thy right assert!
Come, gracious Lord, set up thy throne,
  And reign within my heart!

2 So shall I bless thy pleasing sway,
  And, sitting at thy feet,
Thy laws with all my heart obey,
  With all my soul submit.

3 Thy love the conquest more than gains:
To all I shall proclaim,
Jesus, the King, the Conqueror reigns,
Bow down to Jesus' name.

4 To thee shall earth and hell submit,
And every foe shall fall,
Till death expires beneath thy feet,
And God is all in all.

178   C. M.   (528)

The act of consecration.

LET him to whom we now belong
His sovereign right assert,
And take up every thankful song,
And every loving heart.

2 He justly claims us for his own,
Who bought us with a price:
The Christian lives to Christ alone,
To Christ alone he dies.

3 Jesus, thine own at last receive,
Fulfill our hearts' desire;
And let us to thy glory live,
And in thy cause expire!

4 Our souls and bodies we resign:
With joy we render thee
Our all, no longer ours, but thine,
To all eternity.

179   C. M.   (541)

Longing to be established in love.

O THAT in me the sacred fire
Might now begin to glow!
Burn up the dross of base desire,
And make the mountains flow!

2 O that it now from heaven might fall,
And all my sins consume!
Come, Holy Ghost, for thee I call,
Spirit of burning, come!

3 Refining fire, go through my heart,
Illuminate my soul:
Scatter thy life through every part,
And sanctify the whole.

4 No longer then my heart shall mourn,
While, purified by grace,
I only for his glory burn,
And always see his face.

180   C. M.   (500)

The rapture of love.

I KNOW that my Redeemer lives,
And ever prays for me:
A token of his love he gives,
A pledge of liberty.

2 I find him lifting up my head,
He brings salvation near:
His presence makes me free indeed,
And he will soon appear.

3 He wills that I should holy be!
What can withstand his will?
The counsel of his grace in me
He surely shall fulfill.

4 Jesus, I hang upon thy word:
I steadfastly believe
Thou wilt return, and claim me, Lord,
And to thyself receive.

181   C. M.   (512)

Rejoicing in hope.

O JOYFUL sound of gospel grace!
Christ shall in me appear:

I, even I, shall see his face;
I shall be holy here.

2 The promised land from Pisgah's top
I now exult to see:
My hope is full (O glorious hope!)
Of immortality.

3 With me, I know, I feel, thou art;
But this cannot suffice,
Unless thou plantest in my heart
A constant paradise.

4 Come, O my God, thyself reveal,
Fill all this mighty void:
Thou only canst my spirit fill:
Come, O my God, my God!

82   C. M.   (533)
Praying for a holy heart.

O FOR a heart to praise my God,
A heart from sin set free!
A heart that always feels thy blood
So freely spilt for me!

2 A heart resigned, submissive, meek,
My great Redeemer's throne,
Where only Christ is heard to speak,
Where Jesus reigns alone.

3 O for a lowly, contrite heart,
Believing, true, and clean!
Which neither life nor death can part
From him that dwells within:

4 A heart in every thought renewed,
And full of love divine;
Perfect, and right, and pure, and good—
A copy, Lord, of thine.

183 S. M. (531

The act of consecration.

LORD, in the strength of grace,
With a glad heart and free,
Myself, my residue of days,
I consecrate to thee.

2 Thy ransomed servant, I
Restore to thee thine own;
And, from this moment, live or die,
To serve my God alone.

184 S. M. (493

The new creation.

THE thing my God doth hate,
That I no more may do,
Thy creature, Lord, again create,
And all my soul renew:
My soul shall then, like thine,
Abhor the thing unclean,
And, sanctified by love divine,
Forever cease from sin.

2 That blessèd law of thine,
Jesus, to me impart,
The Spirit's law of life divine,
O write it in my heart!
Implant it deep within,
Whence it may ne'er remove,
The law of liberty from sin,
The perfect law of love.

185 C. M. (540

Longing to be established in love.

MY God! I know, I feel thee mine,
And will not quit my claim,

Till all I have is lost in thine,
And all renewed I am.

2 I hold thee with a trembling hand,
But will not let thee go,
Till steadfastly by faith I stand,
And all thy goodness know.

3 When shall I see the welcome hour,
That plants my God in me!
Spirit of health, and life, and power,
And perfect liberty!

4 Jesus, thine all-victorious love
Shed in my heart abroad;
Then shall my feet no longer rove,
Rooted and fixed in God.

86   S. M.   (546)

Waiting at the Cross.

FATHER, I dare believe
Thee merciful and true:
Thou wilt my guilty soul forgive,
My fallen soul renew.

2 Come, then, for Jesus' sake,
And bid my heart be clean:
An end of all my troubles make,
An end of all my sin.

3 I cannot wash my heart,
But by believing thee,
And waiting for thy blood t' impart
The spotless purity.

4 While at thy cross I lie,
Jesus, thy grace bestow;
Now thy all-cleansing blood apply,
And I am white as snow.

187   7,7,7,7,7,7.   (530)

The act of consecration.

FATHER, Son, and Holy Ghost,
  One in Three, and Three in One,
As by the celestial host,
  Let thy will on earth be done:
Praise by all to thee be given,
Glorious Lord of earth and heaven!

2 If so poor a worm as I
  May to thy great glory live,
All my actions sanctify,
  All my words and thoughts receive:
Claim me for thy service, claim
All I have and all I am.

3 Take my soul and body's powers;
  Take my memory, mind, and will;
All my goods, and all my hours;
  All I know, and all I feel;
All I think, or speak, or do:
Take my heart; but make it new!

188   7s.   (545)

Humble aspiration.

WHEN, my Saviour, shall I be
  Perfectly resigned to thee?
Poor and vile in my own eyes,
Only in thy wisdom wise?

2 Only thee content to know,
Ignorant of all below;
Only guided by thy light;
Only mighty in thy might?

3 So I may thy Spirit know,
Let him as he listeth blow:
Let the manner be unknown,
So I may with thee be one.

4 Fully in my life express
All the heights of holiness:
Sweetly let my spirit prove
All the depths of humble love.

89   7s.   (502)

"Christ liveth in me."

LOVING Jesus, gentle Lamb,
In thy gracious hands I am:
Make me, Saviour, what thou art,
Live thyself within my heart.

2 I shall then show forth thy praise,
Serve thee all my happy days;
Then the world shall always see
Christ, the holy Child, in me.

3. DUTIES AND TRIALS.

90   6,6,8,4.   (552)

The God of Abraham.

THE God of Abrah'm praise,
Who reigns enthroned above,
Ancient of everlasting days,
And God of love:
Jehovah, great I AM!
By earth and heaven confessed;
I bow and bless the sacred Name,
Forever blessed.

2 The God of Abrah'm praise,
At whose supreme command,
From earth I rise, and seek the joys
At his right-hand:
I all on earth forsake,
Its wisdom, fame, and power;
And him my only portion make,
My shield and tower.

3 The God of Abrah'm praise,
Whose all-sufficient grace
Shall guide me all my happy days
In all my ways:
IIe calls a worm his friend!
IIe calls himself my God!
And he shall save me to the end,
Through Jesus' blood!

4 IIe by himself hath sworn;
I on his oath depend;
I shall, on eagles' wings upborne,
To heaven ascend:
I shall behold his face,
I shall his power adore,
And sing the wonders of his grace
Forevermore.

191   7,6,7,6,7,7,7,6.   (556

The pilgrimage.

RISE, my soul, and stretch thy wings,
Thy better portion trace;
Rise from transitory things,
Toward heaven, thy native place:
Sun and moon and stars decay;
Time shall soon this earth remove:
Rise, my soul, and haste away
To seats prepared above.

2 Rivers to the ocean run,
Nor stay in all their course;
Fire ascending seeks the sun—
Both speed them to their source:
So a soul that's born of God
Pants to view his glorious face,
Upward tends to his abode,
To rest in his embrace.

3 Cease, ye pilgrims, cease to mourn;
    Press onward to the prize;
Soon our Saviour will return,
    Triumphant in the skies.
Yet a season, and you know
    Happy entrance will be given;
All our sorrows left below,
    And earth exchanged for heaven.

192   7,6,7,6,7,8,7,6.   (575)

Only Jesus.

VAIN, delusive world, adieu,
    With all of creature-good!
Only Jesus I pursue,
    Who bought me with his blood!
All thy pleasures I forego,
    I trample on thy wealth and pride:
Only Jesus will I know,
    And Jesus crucified.

2 Other knowledge I disdain,
    'T is all but vanity;
Christ, the Lamb of God, was slain,
    He tasted death for me!
Me to save from endless woe
    The sin-atoning Victim died!
Only Jesus will I know,
    And Jesus crucified!

3 O that I could all invite
    This saving truth to prove,
Show the length, the breadth, the height,
    And depth, of Jesus' love!
Fain I would to sinners show
    The blood by faith alone applied!
Only Jesus will I know,
    And Jesus crucified!

193   C. M.   (562

Psalm lxxi. 15.

MY Saviour, my almighty Friend,
   When I begin thy praise,
Where will the growing numbers end,
   The numbers of thy grace?

2 Thou art my everlasting trust;
   Thy goodness I adore:
Send down thy grace, O blessed Lord,
   That I may love thee more.

3 My feet shall travel all the length
   Of the celestial road;
And march with courage in thy strength,
   To see the Lord my God.

4 Awake! awake! my tuneful powers:
   With this delightful song
I'll entertain the darkest hours,
   Nor think the season long.

194   C. M.   (564

Walking with God.

TALK with us, Lord, thyself reveal,
   While here o'er earth we rove;
Speak to our hearts, and let us feel
   The kindlings of thy love.

2 With thee conversing, we forget
   All time, and toil, and care:
Labor is rest, and pain is sweet,
   If thou, my God, art here.

3 Here then, my God, vouchsafe to stay,
   And bid my heart rejoice;
My bounding heart shall own thy sway,
   And echo to thy voice.

4 Thou callest me to seek thy face;
   'T is all I wish to seek:

T' attend the whispers of thy grace,
And hear thee inly speak.

5 Let this my every hour employ,
Till I thy glory see,
Enter into my Master's joy,
And find my heaven in thee!

195   C. M.   (569)

Sluggishness lamented.

MY drowsy powers, why sleep ye so?
  Awake, my sluggish soul!
Nothing hath half thy work to do,
  Yet nothing's half so dull.

2 Go to the ants; for one poor grain
  See how they toil and strive!
Yet we, who have a heaven t' obtain,
  How negligent we live!

3 Lord, shall we live so sluggish still,
  And never act our parts?
Come, Holy Dove, from th' heavenly hill,
  And warm our frozen hearts.

4 Give us with active warmth to move,
  With vigorous souls to rise,
With hands of faith and wings of love
  To fly and take the prize.

196   S. M.   (576)

Depending on Christ.

JESUS, my truth, my way,
  My sure, unerring light,
On thee my feeble steps I stay,
  Which thou wilt guide aright.

2 My wisdom and my guide,
  My counselor thou art:

O never let me leave thy side,
Or from thy paths depart!

3 I lift mine eyes to thee,
Thou gracious, bleeding Lamb,
That I may now enlightened be,
And never put to shame.

4 Never will I remove
Out of thy hands my cause;
But rest in thy redeeming love,
And hang upon thy cross.

197   S. M.   (586
Watchfulness.

GRACIOUS Redeemer, shake
This slumber from my soul!
Say to me now, "Awake, awake!
And Christ shall make thee whole."

2 For each assault prepared
And ready may I be;
Forever standing on my guard,
And looking up to thee.

3 O do thou always warn
My soul of evil near!
When to the right or left I turn,
Thy voice still let me hear:

4 "Come back! this is the way!
Come back! and walk herein!"
O may I hearken and obey,
And shun the paths of sin!

198   S. M.   (587
Concluded.

THOU seest my feebleness:
Jesus, be thou my power,

My help and refuge in distress,
My fortress and my tower.

2 Give me to trust in thee;
Be thou my sure abode:
My horn, and rock, and buckler be,
My Saviour, and my God.

3 Myself I cannot save,
Myself I cannot keep;
But strength in thee I surely have,
Whose eyelids never sleep.

4 My soul to thee alone,
Now, therefore, I commend:
Thou, Jesus, love me as thine own,
And love me to the end!

99   C. M.   (591)
Opening worship.

ONCE more we come before our God;
Once more his blessings ask:
O may not duty seem a load,
Nor worship prove a task!

2 Father, thy quickening Spirit send
From heaven in Jesus' name,
To make our waiting minds attend,
And put our souls in frame.

3 May we receive the word we hear,
Each in an honest heart;
And keep the precious treasure there,
And never with it part.

4 To seek thee all our hearts dispose,
To each thy blessings suit,
And let the seed thy servant sows
Produce abundant fruit.

200 . 7s. (592)

Opening worship.

LORD, we come before thee now,
At thy feet we humbly bow;
O do not our suit disdain!
Shall we seek thee, Lord, in vain?

2 Lord, on thee our souls depend;
In compassion now descend:
Fill our hearts with thy rich grace,
Tune our lips to sing thy praise.

3 In thine own appointed way,
Now we seek thee, here we stay:
Lord, we know not how to go
Till a blessing thou bestow.

4 Send some message from thy word,
That may joy and peace afford;
Let thy Spirit now impart
Full salvation to each heart.

5 Comfort those who weep and mourn,
Let the time of joy return;
Those that are cast down lift up,
Make them strong in faith and hope.

6 Grant that all may seek and find
Thee a gracious God, and kind;
Heal the sick, the captive free;
Let us all rejoice in thee.

201 L. M. (597)

Titus ii. 10–13.

SO let our lips and lives express
The holy gospel we profess;
So let our works and virtues shine,
To prove the doctrine all divine.

2 Thus shall we best proclaim abroad
The honors of our Saviour God,

When the salvation reigns within,
And grace subdues the power of sin.
3 Our flesh and sense must be denied,
Passion and envy, lust and pride;
While justice, temperance, truth, and love,
Our inward piety approve.
4 Religion bears our spirits up,
While we expect that blessed hope,
The bright appearance of the Lord;
And faith stands leaning on his word.

O2 L. M. (589)
Prayer.

PRAYER is appointed to convey
The blessings God designs to give:
Long as they live should Christians pray,
They learn to pray when first they live.

2 If pain afflict, or wrongs oppress;
If cares distract, or fears dismay;
If guilt deject; if sin distress;
In every case still watch and pray.

3 'Tis prayer supports the soul that's weak:
Though thought be broken, language lame
Pray if thou canst or canst not speak,
But pray with faith in Jesus' name.

4 Depend on him; thou canst not fail;
Make all thy wants and wishes known;
Fear not; his merits must prevail;
Ask but in faith, it shall be done.

O3 L. M. (613)
Not ashamed of Jesus.

JESUS! and shall it ever be,
A mortal man ashamed of thee?
Ashamed of thee, whom angels praise,
Whose glories shine through endless days?

5

2 Ashamed of Jesus! sooner far
Let evening blush to own a star:
He sheds the beams of light divine
O'er this benighted soul of mine.

3 Ashamed of Jesus! just as soon
Let midnight be ashamed of noon:
'T is midnight with my soul, till he,
Bright Morning Star, bid darkness flee!

4 Ashamed of Jesus! that dear Friend
On whom my hopes of heaven depend?
No: when I blush, be this my shame, .
That I no more revere his name.

204   L. M.   (605)
At charitable collections.

WHEN Jesus dwelt in mortal clay,
What were his works from day to day,
But miracles of power and grace,
That spread salvation through our race?

2 Teach us, O Lord, to keep in view
.Thy pattern, and thy steps pursue;
Let alms bestowed, let kindness done,
Be witnessed by each rolling sun.

3 That man may *last,* but never *lives,*
Who much receives, but nothing gives,
Whom none can love, whom none can thank,
Creation's blot, creation's blank.

4 But he who marks, from day to day,
In generous acts his radiant way,
Treads the same path the Saviour trod,
The path to glory and to God.

205   L. M.   (625)
Doing all to the glory of God.

O THOU, who camest from above,
The pure celestial fire t' impart,

Kindle a flame of sacred love
On the mean altar of my heart.

2 There let it for thy glory burn,
With inextinguishable blaze,
And trembling to its source return,
In humble love and fervent praise.

3 Jesus, confirm my heart's desire,
To work, and speak, and think, for thee;
Still let me guard the holy fire,
And still stir up thy gift in me.

4 Ready for all thy perfect will,
My acts of faith and love repeat,
Till death thy endless mercies seal,
And make the sacrifice complete.

206   8,7,8,7,4,7.   (558)

The pilgrimage.

GUIDE me, O thou great Jehovah,
  Pilgrim through this barren land;
I am weak, but thou art mighty;
  Hold me with thy powerful hand:
    Bread of heaven,
  Feed me till I want no more.

2 Open, Lord, the crystal fountain
  Whence the healing waters flow;
Let the fiery, cloudy pillar
  Lead me all my journey through:
    Strong Deliverer!
  Be thou still my strength and shield.

3 When I tread the verge of Jordan,
  Bid my anxious fears subside;
Death of death, and hell's destruction,
  Land me safe on Canaan's side:
    Songs of praises
  I will ever give to thee.

207   S. M.   (664)
The triumph.

"I THE good fight have fought,"
      O when shall I declare!
The victory by my Saviour got
   I long with Paul to share.

2 O may I triumph so,
   When all my warfare's past;
And, dying, find my latest foe
   Under my feet at last!

3 This blessed word be mine,
   Just as the port is gained,
"Kept by the power of grace divine,
   I have the faith maintained."

4 Th' apostles of my Lord,
   To whom it first was given,
They could not speak a greater word,
   Nor all the saints in heaven.

208   S. M.   ·   (217 Z.)
The conflict.

MY soul, be on thy guard,
      Ten thousand foes arise:
The hosts of sin are pressing hard
   To draw thee from the skies.

2 O watch, and fight, and pray,
   The battle ne'er give o'er:
Renew it boldly every day,
   And help divine implore.

3 Ne'er think the victory won,
   Nor lay thine armor down:
Thy arduous work will not be done
   Till thou obtain the crown.

4 Fight on, my soul, till death
   Shall bring thee to thy God:
He'll take thee, at thy parting breath,
   Up to his blest abode.

209   S. M.   (594)

Luke xii. 35–37.

YE servants of the Lord,
  Each in his office wait,
Observant of his heavenly word,
  And watchful at his gate.

2 Let all your lamps be bright,
  And trim the golden flame;
Gird up your loins, as in his sight,
  For awful is his name.

3 Watch, 't is your Lord's command;
  And while we speak he's near:
Mark the first signal of his hand,
  And ready all appear.

4 O happy servant he
  In such a posture found!
He shall his Lord with rapture see,
  And be with honor crowned.

210   S. M.   ˉ(657)

Eph. vi. 10.

SOLDIERS of Christ, arise!
  And put your armor on,
Strong in the strength which God supplies
  Through his eternal Son:
Strong in the Lord of hosts,
  And in his mighty power,
Who in the strength of Jesus trusts
  Is more than conqueror.

2 Stand, then, in his great might,
  With all his strength endued;
But take, to arm you for the fight,
  The panoply of God;

That having all things done,
  And all your conflicts passed,
Ye may o'ercome through Christ alone,
  And stand entire at last.

211   C. M.   (209 Z.)

Religion.

RELIGION is the chief concern
  Of mortals here below:
May I its great importance learn,
  Its sovereign virtue know!

2 Religion should our thoughts engage
  Amidst our youthful bloom:
'T will fit us for declining age,
  And for the awful tomb.

3 O may my heart, by grace renewed,
  Be my Redeemer's throne;
And be my stubborn will subdued,
  His government to own!

4 Let deep repentance, faith, and love,
  Be joined with godly fear;
And all my conversation prove
  My heart to be sincere.

5 Let lively hope my soul inspire:
  Let warm affections rise;
And may I wait with strong desire
  To mount above the skies!

212   C. M.   (582)

A tender conscience.

I WANT a principle within
  Of jealous, godly fear,
A sensibility of sin,
  A pain to feel it near.

2 Quick as the apple of an eye,
O God, my conscience make!
Awake my soul when sin is nigh,
And keep it still awake.

3 If to the right or left I stray,
That moment, Lord, reprove;
And let me weep my life away
For having grieved thy love.

4 O may the least omission pain
My well-instructed soul;
And drive me to the blood again
Which makes the wounded whole!

213　　　　C. M.　　　　**(626)**

"Our good is all divine."

FATHER, to thee my soul I lift,
My soul on thee depends,
Convinced that every perfect gift
From thee alone descends.

2 Mercy and grace are thine alone,
And power and wisdom too:
Without the Spirit of thy Son
We nothing good can do.

3 We cannot speak one useful word,
One holy thought conceive,
Unless, in answer to our Lord,
Thyself the blessing give.

4 His blood demands the purchased grace;
His blood's availing plea
Obtained the help for all our race,
And sends it down to me.

5 Thou all our works in us hast wrought;
Our good is all divine:
The praise of every virtuous thought,
And righteous word, is thine.

6 From thee, through Jesus, we receive
  The power on thee to call,
In whom we are, and move, and live:
  Our God is ALL in ALL.

214   C. M.   (619)

Surrendering all for Christ.

HOW vain are all things here below!
  How false, and yet how fair!
Each pleasure hath its poison too,
  And every sweet a snare.

2 The brightest things below the sky
  Give but a flattering light:
We should suspect some danger nigh
  Where we possess delight.

3 Our dearest joys and nearest friends,
  The partners of our blood,
How they divide our wavering minds,
  And leave but half for God!

4 The fondness of a creature's love,
  How strong it strikes the sense!
Thither the warm affections move,
  Nor can we call them thence.

5 Dear Saviour, let thy beauties be
  My soul's eternal food;
And grace command my heart away
  From all created good.

215   C. M.   (611)

Judges v. 31.

JESUS, let all thy lovers shine,
  Illustrious as the sun;
And, bright with borrowed rays divine,
  Their glorious circuit run.

2 Beyond the reach of mortals, spread
  Their light where'er they go;
And heavenly influences shed
  On all the world below.

3 As giants may they run their race,
  Exulting in their might;
As burning luminaries, chase
  The gloom of hellish night.

4 As the bright Sun of righteousness,
  Their healing wings display;
And let their luster still increase
  ·Unto the perfect day.

216   C. M.   (616)

"The Lord is my portion."

MY God, my portion, and my love,
  My everlasting all,
I've none but thee in heaven above,
  Or on this earthly ball.

2 What empty things are all the skies,
  And this inferior clod!
There's nothing here deserves my joys,
  There's nothing like my God.

3 How vain a toy is glittering wealth,
  If once compared to thee!
Or what's my safety, or my health,
  Or all my friends to me?

4 Were I possessor of the earth,
  And called the stars my own,
Without thy graces and thyself,
  I were a wretch undone.

5 Let others stretch their arms like seas,
  And grasp in all the shore:
Grant me the visits of thy face,
  And I desire no more.

217 S. M. (642)

"All things work together for good."

AWAY! my needless fears,
And doubts no longer mine;
A ray of heavenly light appears,
A messenger divine.

2 Thrice comfortable hope,
That calms my troubled breast;
My Father's hand prepares the cup,
And what he wills is best.

3 Here then I doubt no more,
But in his pleasure rest,
Whose wisdom, love, and truth, and power,
Engage to make me blest.

4 T' accomplish his design,
The creatures all agree;
And all the attributes divine
Are now at work for me.

218 S. M. (643)

[From the German of Gerhard.]

Trust in Providence.

COMMIT thou all thy griefs
And ways into his hands,
To his sure trust and tender care,
Who earth and heaven commands:
Who points the clouds their course,
Whom winds and seas obey,
He shall direct thy wandering feet,
He shall prepare thy way.

2 Thou on the Lord rely,
So safe shalt thou go on:
Fix on his work thy steadfast eye,
So shall thy work be done.

No profit canst thou gain
By self-consuming care;
To him commend thy cause, his ear
Attends the softest prayer.

219   S. M.   (644)

Concluded.

GIVE to the winds thy fears;
Hope, and be undismayed:
God hears thy sighs, and counts thy tears
God shall lift up thy head:
Through waves, and clouds, and storms,
He gently clears thy way;
Wait thou his time, so shall this night
Soon end in joyous day.

2 Still heavy is thy heart?
Still sink thy spirits down?
Cast off the weight, let fear depart,
And every care be gone.
What though thou rulest not,
Yet heaven, and earth, and hell
Proclaim, God sitteth on the throne,
And ruleth all things well.

220   S. M.   (607)

Eccles. xi. 6.

SOW in the morn thy seed,
At eve hold not thy hand;
To doubt and fear give thou no heed—
Broad-cast it o'er the land.

2 Thou know'st not which shall thrive,
The late or early sown;
Grace keeps the precious germ alive,
When and wherever strown;

3 And duly shall appear,
In verdure, beauty, strength,

The tender blade, the stalk, the ear,
And the full corn at length.

4 Then, when the final end,
The day of God is come,
The angel reapers shall descend,
And heaven sing, "Harvest home!"

221   S. M.   (621)

Rejoicing in God.

COME, ye that love the Lord,
And let your joys be known:
Join in a song with sweet accord,
While ye surround his throne.

2 Let those refuse to sing
Who never knew our God;
But servants of the heavenly King
May speak their joys abroad.

3 The God that rules on high,
That all the earth surveys,
That rides upon the stormy sky,
And calms the roaring seas—

4 This awful God is ours,
Our Father and our Love;
He will send down his heavenly powers,
To carry us above.

5 There we shall see his face,
And never, never sin;
There, from the rivers of his grace,
Drink endless pleasures in:

6 Then let our songs abound,
And every tear be dry;
We're marching through Immanuel's ground
To fairer worlds on high.

222   C. M.   (612)

"Thou knowest that I love thee."

DO not I love thee, O my Lord?
  Behold my heart, and see;
And turn each cursed idol out
  That dares to rival thee.

2 Do not I love thee from my soul?
  Then let me nothing love;
Dead be my heart to every joy,
  When Jesus cannot move.

3 Hast thou a lamb in all thy flock
  I would disdain to feed?
Hast thou a foe before whose face
  I fear thy cause to plead?

4 Would not my heart pour forth its blood
  In honor of thy name?
And challenge the cold hand of death
  To damp th' immortal flame?

5 Thou know'st I love thee, dearest Lord;
  But O! I long to soar
Far from the sphere of mortal joys,
  And learn to love thee more.

223   C. M.   (638)

Psalm xxxiv. 1–9.

THROUGH all the changing scenes of life,
  In trouble and in joy,
The praises of my God shall still
  My heart and tongue employ.

2 Of his deliverance I will boast,
  Till all that are distressed,
From my example comfort take,
  And charm their griefs to rest.

3 O make but trial of his lov_!
Experience will decide
How blest they are, and only they,
Who in his truth confide.

4 Fear him, ye saints; and you will then
Have nothing else to fear:
Make you his service your delight;
He'll make your wants his care.

224   C. M.   (649)

Contentment.

MY span of life will soon be done,
The passing moments say;
As lengthening shadows o'er the mead
Proclaim the close of day.

2 O that my heart might dwell aloof
From all created things,
And learn that wisdom from above
Whence true contentment springs!

3 Courage, my soul! thy bitter cross,
In every trial here,
Shall bear thee to thy heaven above,
But shall not enter there.

4 The sighing ones that humbly seek
In sorrowing paths below,
Shall in eternity rejoice,
Where endless comforts flow.

5 Soon will the toilsome strife be o'er
Of sublunary care,
And life's dull vanities no more
This anxious breast ensnare.

6 Courage, my soul! on God rely,
Deliverance soon will come:
A thousand ways has Providence
To bring believers home.

225   7s.   (561)

The pilgrim's song.

CHILDREN of the heavenly King,
As we journey, let us sing;
Sing our Saviour's worthy praise,
Glorious in his works and ways.

2 We are traveling home to God,
In the way our fathers trod;
They are happy now, and we
Soon their happiness shall see.

3 O ye banished seed, be glad!
Christ our Advocate is made:
Us to save, our flesh assumes,
Brother to our souls becomes.

4 Fear not, brethren, joyful stand
On the borders of our land;
Jesus Christ, our Father's Son,
Bids us undismayed go on.

5 Lord! obediently we'll go,
Gladly leaving all below:
Only thou our Leader be,
And we still will follow thee.

226   C. M.   (567)

The Christian race.

AWAKE, my soul! stretch every nerve,
And press with vigor on:
A heavenly race demands thy zeal,
And an immortal crown.

2 A cloud of witnesses around
Hold thee in full survey
Forget the steps already trod,
And onward urge thy way.

3 'T is God's all-animating voice
That calls thee from on high;
'T is his own hand presents the prize
To thine aspiring eye:

4 That prize, with peerless glories bright,
Which shall new luster boast,
When victors' wreaths and monarchs' gems
Shall blend in common dust.

5 Blest Saviour! introduced by thee,
Have I my race begun;
And, crowned with victory, at thy feet
I'll lay my honors down.

227   S. M.   (595)
Keeping the charge of the Lord.

A CHARGE to keep I have,
    A God to glorify;
A never-dying soul to save,
    And fit it for the sky;
To serve the present age,
    My calling to fulfill—
O may it all my powers engage
    To do my Master's will!

2 Arm me with jealous care,
    As in thy sight to live;
And O, thy servant, Lord, prepare
    A strict account to give!
Help me to watch and pray,
    And on thyself rely,
Assured if I my trust betray,
    I shall forever die.

228   S. M.   (596)
A holy life.

GOD of almighty love,
    By whose sufficient grace

I lift my heart to things above,
  And humbly seek thy face—
Through Jesus Christ, the just,
  My faint desires receive,
And let me in thy goodness trust,
  And to thy glory live.

2 Whate'er I say or do,
  Thy glory be my aim;
My offerings all be offered through
  The ever-blessèd Name.
Jesus, my single eye
  Be fixed on thee alone;
Thy name be praised on earth, on high,
  Thy will by all be done!

3 Spirit of faith, inspire
  My consecrated heart;
Fill me with pure celestial fire,
  With all thou hast and art.
My feeble mind transform,
  And, perfectly renewed,
Into a saint exalt a worm,
  A worm exalt to God!

229   8,8,6.   (663)
Full assurance of hope.

COME on, my partners in distress,
  My comrades through the wilderness,
    Who still your bodies feel;
Awhile forget your griefs and fears,
And look beyond this vale of tears
    To that celestial hill.

2 Beyond the bounds of time and space
Look forward to that heavenly place,
    The saints' secure abode:
On faith's strong eagle-pinions rise,
And force your passage to the skies,
    And scale the mount of God.

3 Who suffer with our Master here,
We shall before his face appear,
  And by his side sit down:
To patient faith the prize is sure;
And all that to the end endure
  The cross, shall wear the crown.

4 Thrice blessèd, bliss-inspiring hope!
It lifts the fainting spirits up,
  It brings to life the dead:
Our conflicts here shall soon be past,
And you and I ascend at last,
  Triumphant with our Head.

230   8,8,6.   **(580)**

Circumspection.

BE it my only wisdom here
  To serve the Lord with filial fear,
    With loving gratitude;
Superior sense may I display,
By shunning every evil way,
  And walking in the good.

2 O may I still from sin depart;
A wise and understanding heart,
  Jesus, to me be given!
And let me through thy Spirit know
To glorify my God below,
  And find my way to heaven.

231   S. M.   **(624)**

A single eye.

TEACH me, my God and King,
  In all things thee to see;
And what I do, in any thing,
  To do it as for thee;

2 To scorn the senses' sway,
  While still to thee I tend:

In all I do be thou the way,
In all be thou the end.

3 All may of thee partake:
Nothing so small can be,
But draws, when acted for thy sake,
Greatness and worth from thee.

4 If done t' obey thy laws,
E'en servile labors shine;
Hallowed is toil, if this the cause,
The meanest work divine.

5 Thee, then, my God and King,
In all things may I see;
And what I do, in any thing,
May it be done for thee!

32   8,7.   (632)

Taking up the cross.

JESUS, I my cross have taken,
All to leave, and follow thee;
Naked, poor, despised, forsaken,
Thou, from hence, my all shalt be.
Perish, every fond ambition,
All I've sought, or hoped, or known;
Yet how rich is my condition!
God and heaven are still my own!

2 Let the world despise and leave me—
They have left my Saviour too:
Human hearts and looks deceive me—
Thou art not, like them, untrue;
And while thou shalt smile upon me,
God of wisdom, love, and might,
Foes may hate, and friends disown me;
Show thy face, and all is bright.

3 Go, then, earthly fame and treasure;
Come disaster, scorn, and pain;

In thy service pain is pleasure;
With thy favor loss is gain.
I have called thee, Abba, Father,
I have set my heart on thee:
Storms may howl, and clouds may gather—
All must work for good to me.

233   7s.   (630)

Chastisement.

'TIS my happiness below
    Not to live without the cross;
But the Saviour's power to know,
    Sanctifying every loss.

2 Trials must and will befall;
    But with humble faith to see
Love inscribed upon them all—
    This is happiness to me.

3 Trials make the promise sweet;
    Trials give new life to prayer;
Bring me to my Saviour's feet,
    Lay me low, and keep me there.

234   7s.   (647)

Daily bread.

DAY by day the manna fell:
    O, to learn this lesson well!
Still by constant mercy fed,
Give me, Lord, my daily bread.

2 "Day by day," the promise reads,
Daily strength for daily needs:
Cast foreboding fears away;
Take the manna of to-day.

3 Lord! my times are in thy hand:
All my sanguine hopes have planned,

To thy wisdom I resign,
And would make thy purpose mine.

4 Thou my daily task shalt give:
Day by day to thee I live;
So shall added years fulfill,
Not my own, my Father's will.

235　　　8s.　　　(615)

Delight in Christ.

HOW tedious and tasteless the hours
When Jesus no longer I see!
Sweet prospects, sweet birds, and sweet flowers,
Have all lost their sweetness to me:
The midsummer sun shines but dim,
The fields strive in vain to look gay;
But when I am happy in him,
December's as pleasant as May.

2 His name yields the richest perfume,
And sweeter than music his voice;
His presence disperses my gloom,
And makes all within me rejoice:
I should, were he always thus nigh,
Have nothing to wish or to fear;
No mortal so happy as I,
My summer would last all the year.

3 Content with beholding his face,
My all to his pleasure resigned;
No changes of season or place
Would make any change in my mind:
While blessed with a sense of his love,
A palace a toy would appear;
And prisons would palaces prove,
If Jesus would dwell with me there.

4 Dear Lord, if indeed I am thine,
If thou art my sun and my song,
Say why do I languish and pine?
And why are my winters so long?

O drive these dark clouds from my sky,
Thy soul-cheering presence restore;
Or take me to thee up on high,
Where winter and clouds are no more.

236   8s.   (614)

Delight in Christ.

THOU Shepherd of Israel and mine,
The joy and desire of my heart,
For closer communion I pine,
I long to reside where thou art.

2 The pasture I languish to find,
Where all who their Shepherd obey,
Are fed, on thy bosom reclined,
And screened from the heat of the day.

3 'T is there with the lambs of thy flock,
There only I covet to rest;
To lie at the foot of the rock,
Or rise to be hid in thy breast:

4 'T is there I would always abide,
And never a moment depart;
Concealed in the cleft of thy side,
Eternally held in thy heart.

237   8,7.   (623)

Gratitude.

COME, thou Fount of every blessing,
Tune my heart to sing thy grace:
Streams of mercy, never ceasing,
Call for songs of loudest praise.
Teach me some melodious sonnet,
Sung by flaming tongues above;
Praise the mount—I'm fixed upon it—
Mount of thy redeeming love!

2 Here I'll raise mine Ebenezer,
Hither, by thy help, I'm come;

And I hope, by thy good pleasure,
  Safely to arrive at home.
Jesus sought me, when a stranger,
  Wandering from the fold of God:
He, to rescue me from danger,
  Interposed his precious blood!

3 O to grace how great a debtor
  Daily I'm constrained to be!
Let thy goodness, like a fetter,
  Bind my wandering heart to thee!
Prone to wander, Lord, I feel it—
  Prone to leave the God I love—
Here's my heart, O take and seal it!
  Seal it for thy courts above.

238   11s.   (640)

Precious promises.

HOW firm a foundation, ye saints of the Lord,
  Is laid for your faith in his excellent word!
What more can he say than to you he hath said,
You who unto Jesus for refuge have fled?

2 In every condition—in sickness, in health;
In poverty's vale, or abounding in wealth;
At home and abroad; on the land, on the sea—
"As thy days may demand, shall thy strength
    ever be.

3 "Fear not; I am with thee; O be not dis-
    mayed!
I, I am thy God, and will still give thee aid;
I'll strengthen thee, help thee, and cause thee
    to stand,
Upheld by my righteous, omnipotent hand.

4 "When through the deep waters I call thee
    to go,
The rivers of woe shall not thee overflow; .

For I will be with thee, thy troubles to bless,
And sanctify to thee thy deepest distress.

5 "When through fiery trials thy pathway
    shall lie,
My grace, all-sufficient, shall be thy supply:
The flame shall not hurt thee—I only design
Thy dross to consume, and thy gold to refine.

6 " E'en down to old age, all my people shall
    prove
My sovereign, eternal, unchangeable love;
And when hoary hairs shall their temples adorn,
Like lambs they shall still in my bosom be
    borne.

7 "The soul that on Jesus still leans for repose,
I *will* not, I *will* not, desert to his foes;
That soul, though all hell should endeavor to
    shake,
I'll never, *no, never*, NO, NEVER forsake."

239   L. M.   (629)

[From the German.]

Adversity.

O THOU, to whose all-searching sight
  The darkness shineth as the light,
Search, prove my heart, it pants for thee,
O burst these bonds, and set it free!

2 Wash out its stains, refine its dross,
Nail my affections to the cross;
Hallow each thought, let all within
Be clean, as thou, my Lord, art clean.

3 Saviour, where'er thy steps I see,
Dauntless, untired, I follow thee:
O let thy hand support me still,
And lead me to thy holy hill!

4 If rough and thorny be the way,
My strength proportion to my day;
Till toil, and grief, and pain shall cease,
Where all is calm, and joy, and peace.

40　　　　　L. M.　　　　　(639)
Hab. iii. 17, 18.

AWAY, my unbelieving fear!
　Fear shall in me no more have place:
My Saviour doth not yet appear,
　He hides the brightness of his face ;
But shall I therefore let him go,
　And basely to the tempter yield?
No, in the strength of Jesus, no,
　I never will give up my shield.

2 Although the vine its fruit deny,
　Although the olive yield no oil,
The withering fig-tree droop and die,
　The field illude the tiller's toil,
The empty stall no herd afford,
　And perish all the bleating race,
Yet will I triumph in the Lord,　.
　The God of my salvation praise.

41　　　　　C. M.　　　　　(656)
Courage.

AM I a soldier of the cross,
　A follower of the Lamb,
And shall I fear to own his cause,
　Or blush to speak his name?

2 Must I be carried to the skies
　On flowery beds of ease,
While others fought to win the prize,
　And sailed through bloody seas?

3 Are there no foes for me to face?
　Must I not stem the flood ?

Is this vile world a friend to grace,
To help me on to God?

4 Sure I must fight if I would reign;
Increase my courage, Lord:
I'll bear the toil, endure the pain,
Supported by thy word.

5 Thy saints, in all this glorious war,
Shall conquer, though they die;
They see the triumph from afar—
By faith they bring it nigh.

6 When that illustrious day shall rise,
And all thy armies shine,
In robes of victory, through the skies,
The glory shall be thine.

242   C. M.   (654)

Gratitude and hope.

AMAZING grace! (how sweet the sound!)
That saved a wretch like me!
I once was lost, but now I'm found,
Was blind, but now I see.

2 'T was grace that taught my heart to fear,
And grace my fears relieved;
How precious did that grace appear,
The hour I first believed!

3 Through many dangers, toils, and snares,
I have already come;
'T is grace has brought me safe thus far,
And grace will lead me home.

4 The Lord has promised good to me;
His word my hope secures:
He will my shield and portion be
As long as life endures.

5 Yea, when this flesh and heart shall fail,
And mortal life shall cease,
I shall possess within the vail .
A life of joy and peace.

243   C. M.   (655)
Inspiring hope.

WHEN I can read my title clear
   To mansions in the skies,
I'll bid farewell to every fear,
And wipe my weeping eyes.

2 Should earth against my soul engage,
And fiery darts be hurled,
Then I can smile at Satan's rage,
And face a frowning world.

3 Let cares, like a wild deluge, come,
Let storms of sorrow fall;
So I but safely reach my home,
My God, my heaven, my all.

4 There I shall bathe my weary soul
In seas of heavenly rest,
And not a wave of trouble roll
Across my peaceful breast.

SECTION VIII.

Death and the Future State.

244   C. M.   (668)
Psalm xc.

O GOD, our help in ages past,
   Our hope for years to come,
Our shelter from the stormy blast,
And our eternal home:

2 Under the shadow of thy throne,
Still may we dwell secure;
Sufficient is thine arm alone,
And our defense is sure.

3 Before the hills in order stood,
Or earth received her frame,
From everlasting thou art God,
To endless years the same.

4 A thousand ages, in thy sight,
Are like an evening gone;
Short as the watch that ends the night
Before the rising sun.

5 Time, like an ever-rolling stream,
Bears all its sons away;
They fly, forgotten, as a dream
Dies at the opening day.

6 O God, our help in ages past,
Our hope for years to come,
Be thou our guard while life shall last,
And our perpetual home!

245   C. M.   (729

Funeral of a Christian.

WHY do we mourn departing friends,
Or shake at death's alarms?
'T is but the voice that Jesus sends
To call them to his arms.

2 Why should we tremble to convey
Their bodies to the tomb?
There once the flesh of Jesus lay,
And left a long perfume.

3 The graves of all his saints he blessed,
And softened every bed:
Where should the dying members rest,
But with their dying Head?

4 Thence he arose, ascending high,
   And showed our feet the way:
Up to the Lord our flesh shall fly,
   At the great rising day.

5 Then let the last loud trumpet sound,
   And bid our kindred rise:
Awake, ye nations under ground;
   Ye saints, ascend the skies!

246   C. M.   (726)

Funeral of a Christian. Rev. xiv. 13.

HEAR what the voice from heaven proclaims
   For all the pious dead!
Sweet is the savor of their names,
   And soft their sleeping bed.

2 They die in Jesus, and are blessed;
   How kind their slumbers are!
From sufferings and from sins released,
   And freed from every snare.

3 Far from this world of toil and strife,
   They're present with the Lord:
The labors of their mortal life
   End in a large reward.

247   C. M.   (671)

A voice from the tombs.

HARK! from the tombs a doleful sound!
   My ears, attend the cry:
"Ye living men, come view the ground
   Where you must shortly lie.

2 "Princes, this clay must be your bed,
   In spite of all your towers;
The tall, the wise, the reverend head,
   Must lie as low as ours."

3 Great God! is this our certain doom?
And are we still secure?
Still walking downward to the tomb,
And yet prepared no more!

4 Grant us the power of quickening grace,
To fit our souls to fly;
Then, when we drop this dying flesh,
We 'll rise above the sky.

248   L. M.   (678)
Death welcome to the Christian.

SHRINKING from the cold hand of death,
I soon shall gather up my feet;
Shall soon resign this fleeting breath,
And die—my father's God to meet.

2 Numbered among thy people, I
Expect with joy thy face to see:
Because thou didst for sinners die,
Jesus, in death remember me!

3 O that without a lingering groan
I may the welcome word receive!
My body with my charge lay down,
And cease at once to work and live!

4 Walk with me through the dreadful shade,
And, certified that thou art mine,
My spirit, calm and undismayed,
I shall into thy hands resign.

5 No anxious doubt, no guilty gloom,
Shall damp whom Jesus' presence cheers;
My light, my life, my God is come,
And glory in his face appears!

249   L. M.   (679)
The peaceful death.

WHY should we start and fear to die?
What timorous worms we mortals are!

Death is the gate to endless joy,
  And yet we dread to enter there.

2 The pains, the groans, the dying strife,
  Fright our approaching souls away;
And we shrink back again to life,
  Fond of our prison and our clay.

3 O if my Lord would come and meet,
  My soul would stretch her wings in haste,
Fly fearless through death's iron gate,
  Nor feel the terrors as she passed!

4 Jesus can make a dying-bed
  Feel soft as downy pillows are,
While on his breast I lean my head,
  And breathe my life out sweetly there.

250   L. M.   (693)
Dies iræ.

THE day of wrath, that dreadful day,
  When heaven and earth shall pass away!
What power shall be the sinner's stay?
How shall he meet that dreadful day—

2 When, shriveling like a parchèd scroll,
The flaming heavens together roll;
And louder yet, and yet more dread,
Swells the high trump that wakes the dead?

3 O on that day, that wrathful day,
When man to judgment wakes from clay,
Be thou, O Christ, the sinner's stay,
Though heaven and earth shall pass away!

251   L. M.   (697)
Heaven. Psalm xvii. 15.

WHAT sinners value I resign;
  Lord, 't is enough that thou art mine:

I shall behold thy blissful face,
And stand complete in righteousness.

2 This life's a dream, an empty show;
But the bright world to which I go
Hath joys substantial and sincere:
· When shall I wake and find me there?

3 O glorious hour! O blest abode!
I shall be near, and like, my God;
And flesh and sin no more control
The sacred pleasures of the soul.

4 My flesh shall slumber in the ground
Till the last trumpet's joyful sound;
Then burst the chains with sweet surprise,
And in my Saviour's image rise.

252   C. M.   (720)

Funeral of a child.

THY life I read, my gracious Lord,
   With transport all divine:
Thine image trace in every word,
   Thy love in every line.

2 Methinks I see a thousand charms
   Spread o'er thy lovely face,
While infants in thy tender arms
   Receive the smiling grace.

3 "I take these little lambs," said he,
   "And lay them in my breast:
Protection they shall find in me,
   In me be ever blest.

4 "Death may the bands of life unloose,
   But can't dissolve my love:
Millions of infant souls compose
   The family above."

253 C. M. (721)

Funeral of a child.

L IFE is a span, a fleeting hour:
How soon the vapor flies!
Man is a tender, transient flower,
That e'en in blooming dies.

2 Death spreads his withering, wintry arms,
And beauty smiles no more:
Ah! where are now those rising charms
Which pleased our eyes before?

3 That once loved form, now cold and dead,
Each mournful thought employs;
We weep our earthly comforts fled,
And withered all our joys.

4 Hope looks beyond the bounds of time,
When what we now deplore
Shall rise in full, immortal prime,
And bloom to fade no more.

254 C. M. (688)

The saints above.

G IVE me the wings of faith, to rise
Within the vail, and see
The saints above, how great their joys,
How bright their glories be.

2 I ask them whence their victory came:
They, with united breath,
Ascribe their conquest to the Lamb,
Their triumph to his death.

3 They marked the footsteps that he trod
His zeal inspired their breast;
And, following their incarnate God,
Possess the promised rest.

6

4 Our glorious Leader claims our praise
· For his own pattern given;
While the long cloud of witnesses
   Show the same path to heaven.

255   **L. M.**   **(724)**

Funeral of a youth. 1 *Peter* i. 24, 25.

THE morning flowers display their sweets,
   And gay their silken leaves unfold,
As careless of the noontide heats,
   As fearless of the evening cold.

2 Nipped by the wind's unkindly blast,
   Parched by the sun's directer ray,
The momentary glories waste,
   The short-lived beauties die away.

3 So blooms the human face divine,
   When youth its pride of beauty shows:
Fairer than spring the colors shine,
   And sweeter than the virgin rose.

4 Or worn by slowly-rolling years,
   Or broke by sickness in a day,
The fading glory disappears,
   The short-lived beauties die away.

5 Yet these, new-rising from the tomb,
   With luster brighter far shall shine,
Revive with ever-during bloom,
   Safe from diseases and decline.

6 Let sickness blast, let death devour,
   If heaven must recompense our pains:
Perish the grass, and fade the flower,
   If firm the word of God remains.

256   **L. M.**   **(728)**

Funeral of a Christian.

UNVEIL thy bosom, faithful tomb,
   Take this new treasure to thy trust;

And give these sacred relics room,
To slumber in the silent dust.

2 Nor pain, nor grief, nor anxious fear,
Invades thy bounds; no mortal woes
Can reach the peaceful sleeper here,
While angels watch the soft repose.

3 So Jesus slept: God's dying Son
Passed through the grave, and blessed the bed:
Rest here, blest saint, till from his throne
The morning break, and pierce the shade.

4 Break from his throne, illustrious morn!
Attend, O earth, his sovereign word!
Restore thy trust: a glorious form
Shall then arise to meet the Lord.

257   L. M.   (681)
Death of the righteous.

HOW blest the righteous when he dies!
When sinks a weary soul to rest,
How mildly beam the closing eyes!
How gently heaves th' expiring breast!

2 So fades a summer cloud away;
So sinks the gale when storms are o'er;
So gently shuts the eye of day;
So dies a wave along the shore.

3 Life's duty done, as sinks the clay,
Light from its load the spirit flies;
While heaven and earth combine to say,
"How blest the righteous when he dies!"

258   C. M.   (669)
Brevity of life.

THEE we adore, eternal Name!
And humbly own to thee

How feeble is our mortal frame,
  What dying worms we be!

2 The year rolls round, and steals away
  The breath that first it gave:
Whate'er we do, where'er we be,
  We're traveling to the grave.

3 Dangers stand thick through all the ground
  To push us to the tomb;
And fierce diseases wait around
  To hurry mortals home.

4 Waken, O Lord, our drowsy sense
  To walk this dangerous road;
And if our souls be hurried hence,
  May they be found with God!

259   C. M.   (719)

Eternal death.

THAT awful day will surely come,
  Th' appointed hour makes haste,
When I must stand before my Judge,
  And pass the solemn test.

2 Jesus, thou Source of all my joys,
  Thou Ruler of my heart,
How could I bear to hear thy voice
  Pronounce the sound, "Depart!"

3 The thunder of that awful word
  Would so torment my ear,
'T would tear my soul asunder, Lord,
  With most tormenting fear.

4 O wretched state of deep despair,
  To see my God remove,
And fix my doleful station where
  I must not taste his love!

260   C. M.   (689)

The day of judgment.

AND must I be to judgment brought,
   And answer in that day
For every vain and idle thought,
   And every word I say?

2 Yes, every secret of my heart
   Shall shortly be made known,
And I receive my just desert
   For all that I have done.

3 How careful, then, ought I to live!
   With what religious fear!
Who such a strict account must give
   For my behavior here!

4 Thou awful Judge of quick and dead,
   The watchful power bestow;
So shall I to my ways take heed,
   To all I speak or do.

5 If now thou standest at the door,
   O let me feel thee near!
And make my peace with God, before
   I at thy bar appear.

261   S. M.   (298 ‡ .

Peaceful death.

O FOR the death of those
   Who slumber in the Lord!
O be, like theirs, my last repose,
   Like theirs my last reward!

2 Their bodies in the ground
   In silent hope may lie,
Till the last trumpet's joyful sound
   Shall call them to the sky.

3 Their ransomed spirits soar,
   On wings of faith and love,
To meet the Saviour they adore,
   And reign with him above.

4 With us their names shall live
   Through long succeeding years,
Embalmed with all our hearts can give,
   Our praises and our tears.

5 O for the death of those,
   Who slumber in the Lord!
O be, like theirs, my last repose,
   Like theirs my last reward!

262   S. M.   (730)
Funeral of a Christian.

AND must this body die,
   This well-wrought frame decay?
And must these active limbs of mine
   Lie moldering in the clay?

2 Corruption, earth, and worms,
   Shall but refine this flesh,
Till my triumphant spirit comes
   To put it on afresh.

3 Arrayed in glorious grace
   Shall these vile bodies shine,
And every shape, and every face,
   Be heavenly and divine.

4 These lively hopes we owe,
   Lord, to thy dying love:
O may we bless thy grace below,
   And sing thy grace above!

263   • S. M.   (676)
The issues of life and death.

O WHERE shall rest be found,
   Rest for the weary soul?

'T were vain the ocean-depths to sound,
  Or pierce to either pole:

2 The world can never give
  The bliss for which we sigh:
'T is not the whole of life to live,
  Nor all of death to die.

3 Beyond this vale of tears
  There is a life above,
Unmeasured by the flight of years;
  And all that life is love:

4 There is a death whose pang
  Outlasts the fleeting breath;
O what eternal horrors hang
  Around "the second death!"

5 Lord God of truth and grace,
  Teach us that death to shun,
Lest we be banished from thy face,
  And evermore undone.

264   S. M.   (674)

The end of life.

AND am I born to die?
  To lay this body down?
And must my trembling spirit fly
  Into a world unknown?

2 A land of deepest shade,
  Unpierced by human thought;
The dreary regions of the dead,
  Where all things are forgot!

3 Soon as from earth I go,
  What will become of me?
Eternal happiness or woe
  Must then my portion be.

4 Waked by the trumpet's sound,
  I from my grave shall rise;
And see the Judge with glory crowned,
  And see the flaming skies!
5 Who can resolve the doubt
  That tears my anxious breast?
Shall I be with the damned cast out,
  Or numbered with the blest?
6 I must from God be driven,
  Or with my Saviour dwell;
Must come at his command to heaven,
  Or else—depart to hell.

265   S. M.   (675)
The end of life.

O THOU that wouldst not have
  One wretched sinner die;
Who diedst thyself, my soul to save
  From endless misery!
2 Show me the way to shun
  Thy dreadful wrath severe;
That when thou comest on thy throne,
  I may with joy appear!
3 Thou art thyself the way,
  Thyself in me reveal;
So shall I spend my life's short day
  Obedient to thy will:
4 So shall I love my God,
  Because he first loved me;
And praise thee in thy bright abode
  To all eternity.

266   C. M.   (705)
The heavenly Jerusalem.

JERUSALEM, my happy home!
  Name ever dear to me!

When shall my labors have an end,
  In joy, and peace, and thee?

2 O when, thou city of my God,
  Shall I thy courts ascend,
Where congregations ne'er break up,
  And Sabbaths have no end?

3 Why should I shrink at pain and woe?
  Or feel at death dismay?
I've Canaan's goodly land in view,
  And realms of endless day.

4 Jerusalem! my happy home!
  My soul still pants for thee;
Then shall my labors have an end,
  When I thy joys shall see.

267   C. M.   (706)
The heavenly Canaan.

THERE is a land of pure delight,
  Where saints immortal reign;
Infinite day excludes the night,
  And pleasures banish pain.

2 There everlasting spring abides,
  And never-withering flowers:
Death, like a narrow sea, divides
  This heavenly land from ours.

3 Sweet fields beyond the swelling flood
  Stand dressed in living green:
So to the Jews old Canaan stood,
  While Jordan rolled between.

4 Could we but climb where Moses stood,
  And view the landscape o'er,
Not Jordan's stream, nor death's cold flood,
  Should fright us from the shore.

268 C. M. (707)

The heavenly Canaan.

ON Jordan's stormy banks I stand,
  And cast a wishful eye
To Canaan's fair and happy land,
  Where my possessions lie.

2 O the transporting, rapturous scene,
  That rises to my sight!
Sweet fields arrayed in living green,
  And rivers of delight!

3 There generous fruits that never fail
  On trees immortal grow;
There rocks, and hills, and brooks, and vales,
  With milk and honey flow.

4 All o'er those wide-extended plains
  Shines one eternal day;
There God, the Sun, forever reigns,
  And scatters night away.

5 No chilling winds nor poisonous breath
  Can reach that healthful shore;
Sickness and sorrow, pain and death,
  Are felt and feared no more.

6 When shall I reach that happy place,
  And be forever blest?
When shall I see my Father's face,
  And in his bosom rest?

7 Filled with delight, my raptured soul
  Would here no longer stay!
Though Jordan's waves around me roll,
  Fearless I'd launch away.

269 8,8,6. (673)

The end of life.

AND am I only born to die?
  And must I suddenly comply
With nature's stern decree?

What after death for me remains?
Celestial joys or hellish pains,
  To all eternity!

2 No room for mirth or trifling here,
For worldly hope or worldly fear,
  If life so soon is gone;
If now the Judge is at the door,
And all mankind must stand before
  Th' inexorable throne!

3 Nothing is worth a thought beneath,
But how I may escape the death
  That never, never dies!
How make mine own election sure,
And when I fail on earth, secure
  A mansion in the skies.

4 Jesus, vouchsafe a pitying ray,
Be thou my guide, be thou my way,
  To glorious happiness!
Ah! write the pardon on my heart!
And whensoe'er I hence depart,
  Let me depart in peace!

270   7s.   (702)
        Rev. vii. 13–17.

WHAT are these arrayed in white,
  Brighter than the noonday sun;
Foremost of the sons of light,
  Nearest the eternal throne?
These are they that bore the cross,
  Nobly for their Master stood;
Sufferers in his righteous cause,
  Followers of the dying God.

2 Out of great distress they came,
  Washed their robes by faith below
In the blood of yonder Lamb,
  Blood that washes white as snow; .

Therefore are they next the throne,
  Serve their Maker day and night:
God resides among his own,
  God doth in his saints delight.

271   C. M.   (713, 715)
  The full assurance of hope.

HOW happy every child of grace,
  Who knows his sins forgiven!
This earth, he cries, is not my place,
  I seek my place in heaven;
A country far from mortal sight—
  Yet, O! by faith I see
The land of rest, the saints' delight,
  The heaven prepared for me.

2 O what a blessèd hope is ours!
  While here on earth we stay,
We more than taste the heavenly powers,
  And antedate that day:
We feel the resurrection near,
  Our life in Christ concealed,
And with his glorious presence here
  Our earthen vessels filled.

3 O would he more of heaven bestow,
  And let the vessels break,
And let our ransomed spirits go,
  To grasp the God we seek;
In rapturous awe on him to gaze,
  Who bought the sight for me,
And shout, and wonder at his grace,
  To all eternity!

272   C. M.   (711, 712)
  Visions of heaven.

AND let this feeble body fail,
  And let it droop or die:

My soul shall quit the mournful vale,
 And soar to worlds on high—
Shall join the disembodied saints,
 And find its long-sought rest,
That only bliss for which it pants,
 In my Redeemer's breast.

2 In hope of that immortal crown,
 I now the cross sustain;
And gladly wander up and down,
 And smile at toil and pain:
I suffer out my three-score years,
 Till my Deliverer come,
And wipe away his servant's tears,
 And take his exile home.

3 O what are all my sufferings here,
 If, Lord, thou count me meet
With that enraptured host t' appear,
 And worship at thy feet!
Give joy or grief, give ease or pain—
 Take life or friends away,
I come to find them all again
 In that eternal day.

273   C. M.   (716)
The whole family in heaven and earth.

COME, let us join our friends above,
 That have obtained the prize;
And on the eagle wings of love
 To joys celestial rise:
Let all the saints terrestrial sing,
 With those to glory gone;
For all the servants of our King,
 In earth and heaven, are one.

2 One family we dwell in him,
 One Church above, beneath,
Though now divided by the stream,
 The narrow stream, of death.

One army of the living God,
  To his command we bow;
Part of his host have crossed the flood,
  And part are crossing now.

3 Our old companions in distress
  We haste again to see,
And eager long for our release
  And full felicity:
E'en now by faith we join our hands
  With those that went before,
And greet the blood-besprinkled bands
  On the eternal shore.

274   S. M.   (347 Z.)

Forever with the Lord.

" FOREVER with the Lord!"
  Amen, so let it be:
Life from the dead is in that word,
  'T is immortality.
Here, in the body pent,
  Absent from him I roam;
Yet nightly pitch my moving tent
  A day's march nearer home.

2 My Father's house on high,
  Home of my soul, how near,
At times, to faith's foreseeing eye,
  Thy golden gates appear.
Yet clouds will intervene,
  And all my prospect flies:
Like Noah's dove I flit between
  Rough seas and stormy skies.

3 Anon the clouds dispart,
  The winds and waters cease,
While sweetly o'er my gladdened heart
  Expands the bow of peace.

Beneath its glowing arch,
Along the hallowed ground,
I see cherubic armies march,
A camp of fire around.

275   11s.   (708)
"I would not live alway."

I WOULD not live alway: I ask not to stay
  Where storm after storm rises dark o'er the
    way;
The few lurid mornings that dawn on us here
Are enough for life's woes, full enough for its
    cheer.

2 I would not live alway: no—welcome the
    tomb;
Since Jesus hath lain there, I dread not its
    gloom:
There sweet be my rest till he bid me arise,
To hail him in triumph descending the skies.

3 Who, who would live alway, away from his
    God,
Away from yon heaven, that blissful abode,
Where the rivers of pleasure flow o'er the bright
    plains,
And the noontide of glory eternally reigns:

4 Where the saints of all ages in harmony
    meet,
Their Saviour and brethren transported to
    greet;
While the anthems of rapture unceasingly roll,
And the smile of the Lord is the feast of the
    soul!

276   8,7.   (513 Z.)
There is rest for the weary.

IN the Christian's home in glory,
  There remains a land of rest:

There my Saviour's gone before me,
To fulfill my soul's request.

Chorus.—There is rest for the weary—
There is rest for the weary—
There is rest for the weary—
There is rest for you—
On the other side of Jordan,
In the sweet fields of Eden,
Where the tree of life is blooming—
There is rest for you.

2 He is fitting up my mansion,
Which eternally shall stand,
For my stay shall not be transient
In that holy, happy land.

3 Pain and sickness ne'er shall enter,
Grief nor woe my lot shall share,
But, in that celestial center,
I a crown of life shall wear.

4 Death itself shall there be vanished,
And his sting shall be withdrawn;
Shout for gladness, O ye ransomed,
Hail with joy the rising dawn!

5 Sing, O sing, ye heirs of glory—
Shout your triumphs as ye go;
Zion's gates will open for you,
Ye shall find an entrance through.

277   13,11.   (731)

Funeral of a Christian.

THOU art gone to the grave—but we will not
deplore thee:
Though sorrows and darkness encompass the
tomb,

Thy Saviour has passed through its portal before thee,
And the lamp of his love is thy guide through
the gloom.

2 Thou art gone to the grave—we no longer
behold thee,
Nor tread the rough paths of the world by
thy side;
But the wide arms of mercy.are spread to en-
fold thee,
And sinners may die since the Sinless has
died.

3 Thou art gone to the grave—and its mansion forsaking,
Perchance thy weak spirit in fear lingered
long;
But the mild rays of paradise beamed on thy
waking,
And the sound which thou heardst was the
seraphim's song.

4 Thou art gone to the grave—but we will not
deplore thee,
Whose God was thy ransom, thy guardian,
and guide;
He gave thee; he took thee; and he will restore thee;
And death has no sting, for the Saviour has
died.

278   S. M.   (739)

Funeral of an aged minister.

"SERVANT of God, well done!
Rest from thy loved employ;
The battle fought, the victory won,
Enter thy Master's joy."

2 The voice at midnight came;
  He started up to hear;
A mortal arrow pierced his frame:
  He fell; but felt no fear.

3 The pains of death are past,
  Labor and sorrow cease;
And, life's long warfare closed at last,
  His soul is found in peace.

4 Soldier of Christ, well done!
  Praise be thy new employ;
And while eternal ages run,
  Rest in thy Saviour's joy.

279   S. M.   (524 Z.)

Nearing the end.

ONE sweetly solemn thought
  Comes to me o'er and o'er:
Nearer my parting hour am I
  Than e'er I was before.

2 Nearer my Father's house,
  Where many mansions be;
Nearer the throne where Jesus reigns—
  Nearer the crystal sea;

3 Nearer my going home,
  Laying my burden down,
Leaving my cross of heavy grief,
  Wearing my starry crown;

4 Nearer that hidden stream,
  Winding through shades of night,
Rolling its cold, dark waves between
  Me and the world of light.

5 Jesus! to thee I cling:
  Strengthen my arm of faith;
Stay near me while my way-worn feet
  Press through the stream of death.

SECTION IX.
Special Occasions.

1. MISSIONS.

280   L. M.   (741)

Psalm lxxii.

JESUS shall reign where'er the sun
Does his successive journeys run;
His kingdom stretch from shore to shore,
Till moons shall wax and wane no more.

2 From north to south the princes meet
To pay their homage at his feet;
While western empires own their Lord,
And savage tribes attend his word.

3 For him shall endless prayer be made,
And endless praises crown his head;
His name, like sweet perfume, shall rise
With every morning sacrifice.

4 People and realms, of every tongue,
Dwell on his love with sweetest song,
And infant voices shall proclaim
Their early blessings on his name.

5 Blessings abound where'er he reigns,
The prisoner leaps to loose his chains,
The weary find eternal rest,
And all the sons of want are blessed.

6 Where he displays his healing power,
Death and the curse are known no more:
In him the tribes of Adam boast
More blessings than their father lost.

7 Let every creature rise and bring
Peculiar honors to our King;
Angels descend with songs again,
And earth repeat the long Amen!

281   L. M.   (744)
Psalm cxvii.

FROM all that dwell below the skies,
  Let the Creator's praise arise;
Let the Redeemer's name be sung
Through every land, by every tongue.

2 Eternal are thy mercies, Lord,
Eternal truth attends thy word;
Thy praise shall sound from shore to shore
Till suns shall rise and set no more.

282   8,7,4.   (266 Z.)
Isa. lii. 7.

ON the mountain's top appearing,
  Lo, the sacred herald stands,
Welcome news to Zion bearing,
  Zion long in hostile lands:
    Mourning captive,
  God himself will loose thy bands.

2 Has thy night been long and mournful,
  All thy friends unfaithful proved?
Have thy foes been proud and scornful,
  By thy sighs and tears unmoved?
    Cease thy mourning,
  Zion still is well beloved.

3 God, thy God, will now restore thee!
  He himself appears thy friend:
All thy foes shall flee before thee,
  Here their boasts and triumphs end:
    Great deliverance
  Zion's King vouchsafes to send.

283   8,7,8,7,4,7.   (756)

Spread of the gospel.

O'ER the gloomy hills of darkness,
  Look, my soul, be still and gaze,
All thy promises do travail
  With a glorious day of grace:
    Blessèd jubilee,
  Let thy glorious morning dawn!

2 Kingdoms wide that sit in darkness,
  Grant them, Lord, the glorious light,
And from eastern coast to western,
  May the morning chase the night;
    And redemption,
  Freely purchased, win the day.

3 Fly abroad, thou mighty gospel;
  Win and conquer, never cease;
May thy lasting, wide dominions
  Multiply, and still increase:
    Sway thy scepter,
  Saviour, all the world around.

284   7s.   (767)

Success.

SEE how great a flame aspires,
  Kindled by a spark of grace!
Jesus' love the nations fires,
  Sets the kingdoms on a blaze.
To bring fire on earth he came;
  Kindled in some hearts it is:
O that all might catch the flame,
  All partake the glorious bliss!

2 When he first the work begun,
  Small and feeble was his day:
Now the word doth swiftly run,
  Now it wins its widening way:

More and more it spreads and grows,
  Ever mighty to prevail;
Sin's strongholds it now o'erthrows,
  Shakes the trembling gates of hell.

3 Saw ye not the cloud arise,
  Little as a human hand?
Now it spreads along the skies,
  Hangs o'er all the thirsty land;
Lo! the promise of a shower
  Drops already from above;
But the Lord will shortly pour
  All the Spirit of his love.

285   7s.   (765)

"Watchman, what of the night?"

WATCHMAN, tell us of the night,
  What its signs of promise are.
Traveler, o'er yon mountain's height,
  See that glory-beaming star.
Watchman, does its beauteous ray
  Aught of hope or joy foretell?
Traveler, yes; it brings the day,
  Promised day of Israel.

2 Watchman, tell us of the night:
  Higher yet that star ascends.
Traveler, blessedness and light,
  Peace and truth, its course portends.
Watchman, will its beams alone
  Gild the spot that gave them birth?
Traveler, ages are its own;
  See! it bursts o'er all the earth.

3 Watchman, tell us of the night,
  For the morning seems to dawn.
Traveler, darkness takes its flight,
  Doubt and terror are withdrawn.

Watchman, let thy wanderings cease;
  Hie thee to thy quiet home.
Traveler, lo! the Prince of peace,
  Lo! the Son of God is come.

286   7,6,7,6.   (760)

"Come over—and help us!"

FROM Greenland's icy mountains,
  From India's coral strand;
Where Afric's sunny fountains
  Roll down their golden sand;
From many an ancient river,
  From many a palmy plain,
They call us to deliver
  Their land from error's chain.

2 What though the spicy breezes
  Blow soft o'er Ceylon's isle,
Though every prospect pleases,
  And only man is vile:
In vain with lavish kindness
  The gifts of God are strown;
The heathen in his blindness
  Bows down to wood and stone.

3 Shall we whose souls are lighted
  With wisdom from on high,
Shall we to men benighted
  The lamp of life deny?
Salvation! O salvation!
  The joyful sound proclaim,
Till earth's remotest nation
  Has learned Messiah's name.

4 Waft, waft, ye winds, his story,
  And you, ye waters, roll,
Till, like a sea of glory,
  It spreads from pole to pole:

Till o'er our ransomed nature
The Lamb for sinners slain,
Redeemer, King, Creator,
In bliss returns to reign.

2. BIBLE.

287   L. M.   (770)

Psalm xix.

THE heavens declare thy glory, Lord,
In every star thy wisdom shines;
But when our eyes behold thy word,
We read thy name in fairer lines.

2 The rolling sun, the changing light,
And night and day, thy power confess;
But the blest volume thou hast writ,
Reveals thy justice and thy grace.

3 Sun, moon, and stars, convey thy praise
Round the whole earth, and never stand;
So when thy truth began its race,
It touched and glanced on every land.

4 Nor shall thy spreading gospel rest,
Till through the world thy truth has run:
Till Christ has all the nations blessed,
That see the light, or feel the sun.

5 Great Sun of righteousness, arise!
Bless the dark world with heavenly light:
Thy gospel makes the simple wise:
Thy laws are pure, thy judgments right.

288   C. M.   (771)

Psalm cxix.

HOW shall the young secure their hearts,
And guard their lives from sin?
Thy word the choicest rule imparts
To keep the conscience clean.

2 When once it enters to the mind,
  It spreads such light abroad,
The meanest souls instruction find,
  And raise their thoughts to God.
3 'T is like the sun, a heavenly light,
  That guides us all the day;
And through the dangers of the night,
  A lamp to lead our way.
4 Thy word is everlasting truth;
  How pure is every page!
That holy book shall guide our youth,
  And well support our age.

289   L. M.   (772)
Excellence of God's word.

L ET everlasting glories crown
  Thy head, my Saviour, and my Lord;
Thy hands have brought salvation down,
And writ the blessings in thy word.
2 In vain the trembling conscience seeks
  Some solid ground to rest upon;
With long despair the spirit breaks,
  Till we apply to Christ alone.
3 How well thy blessèd truths agree!
  How wise and holy thy commands!
Thy promises, how firm they be!
How firm our hope, our comfort, stands!
4 Should all the forms that men devise
  Assault my faith with treacherous art,
I'd call them vanity and lies,
  And bind the gospel to my heart.

3. ERECTION OF CHURCHES.

290   L. M.   (786)
Psalm lxxxvii.

A ND will the great, eternal God,
  On earth establish his abode?

And will he from his radiant throne,
Avow our temple for his own?

2 We bring the tribute of our praise;
And sing that condescending grace,
Which to our notes will lend an ear,
And call us sinful mortals near.

3 These walls we to thy honor raise,
Long may they echo to thy praise;
And thou, descending, fill the place
With choicest tokens of thy grace.

4 And in the great, decisive day,
When God the nations shall survey,
May it before the world appear
That crowds were born to glory here!

291   C. M.   (782)
Psalm cxviii. 22, 23.

BEHOLD the sure foundation-stone
Which God in Zion lays,
To build our heavenly hopes upon,
And his eternal praise.

2 Chosen of God, to sinners dear,
We now adore thy name;
We trust our whole salvation here,
Nor can we suffer shame.

3 The foolish builders, scribe and priest,
Reject it with disdain;
Yet on this Rock the Church shall rest,
And envy rage in vain.

4 What though the gates of hell withstood,
Yet must this building rise:
'T is thine own work, Almighty God,
And wondrous in our eyes.

292   S. M.   (788)

Psalm xlviii.

GREAT is the Lord our God,
  And let his praise be great;
He makes his churches his abode,
  His most delightful seat.

2 These temples of his grace,
  How beautiful they stand!
The honors of our native place,
  And bulwarks of our land.

3 In Sion God is known
  A refuge in distress:
How bright has his salvation shone
  Through all her palaces!

4 In every new distress
  We'll to his house repair;
We'll think upon his wondrous grace,
  And seek deliverance there.

4. EDUCATION OF YOUTH.

293   L. M.

Laying a corner-stone of an institution.

ALMIGHTY God, we to thy praise,
  And in thy name, this building raise;
Here shall thy wondrous works be shown,
And here thy sovereign will made known.

2 Science and Revelation here
In perfect harmony appear,
Guiding young feet along the road,
Through grace and nature up to God.

3 Sons of the prophets here shall be
Taught in thy way more perfectly,
That others they in turn may teach
The mysteries they are called to preach.

4 In thy great name, O Lord, alone,
We this day lay our corner-stone:
O let thy work to us appear—
Thy glory to our seed declare!

5 Praise to the Father, and the Son,
And Holy Spirit—three in one;
As 't was of old, is now, shall be,
Ascribed to all eternity!

294   L. M.

Commencement ode.

FATHER of lights! with one accord,
 Thy works and word proclaim thee Lord—
Reveal thy wisdom, power, and love,
To all around, beneath, above.

2 By faith and science here we trace
Thee, God of nature, and of grace:
Though dimly seen, yet seen art thou—
Father of lights! we see thee now!

3 But when we gain that world of bliss,
Where faith and science both shall cease,
Where floods of light burst from thy throne,
Then shall we know as we are known.

4 JEHOVAH ELOHIM! to thee—
In essence one, in persons three—
With bounding heart, and tuneful tongue,
We raise our glad Commencement-song!

295   6,6,4,6,6,6,4.

Commencement ode.

FATHER of lights! thy name
 This glad day we proclaim,
With bounding heart:

Ancient of endless days,
Thy works declare thy praise—
Thy word, with brighter rays,
   Shows what thou art.

2 Open our eyes that we
Thy glory, Lord, may see
   In thy own light:
That glory may we trace
In all the truth and grace,
Which beams in Jesus' face—
   Transporting sight!

3 Hear us, Lord God of truth,
Shine forth upon our youth—
   We humbly pray:
Let them thy influence prove—
Spirit of light and love,
Beam on them from above
   This festal day!

296   C. M.   (800)
For an orphan asylum.

FATHER of mercies, hear our prayers
   For those that do us good,
Whose love for us a place prepares,
   And gives the orphans food.

2 Their alms in blessings on their head
   A thousand-fold restore;
O feed their souls with living bread,
   And let their cup run o'er!

3 Forever in thy Christ built up,
   Thy bounty let them prove;
Steadfast in faith, joyful through hope,
   And rooted deep in love.

4 For those who kindly founded this,
   A better house prepare;
Remove them to thy heavenly bliss,
   And let us meet them there.

5. THE SEASONS.

297   10,5,11.   (803)

New-year's-day.

COME, let us anew Our journey pursue,
Roll round with the year,
And never stand still till the Master appear!
His adorable will Let us gladly fulfill,
And our talents improve,
By the patience of hope, and the labor of love.

2 Our life is a dream; Our time, as a stream,
Glides swiftly away;
And the fugitive moment refuses to stay. ~
The arrow is flown, The moment is gone;
The millennial year
Rushes on to our view, and eternity's here.

3 O that each in the day Of his coming may say,
"I have fought my way through;
I have finished the work thou didst give me
to do!"
O that each from his Lord May receive the
glad word,
"Well and faithfully done!
Enter into my joy, and sit down on my throne."

298   C. M.   (808)

New-year's-day.

SING to the great Jehovah's praise!
All praise to him belongs,
Who kindly lengthens out our days,
Demands our choicest songs:
His providence hath brought us through
Another various year;
We all with vows and anthems new
Before our God appear.

2 Father, thy mercies past we own,
Thy still continued care;
To thee presenting, through thy Son,
Whate'er we have or are:
Our lips and lives shall gladly show
The wonders of thy love,
While on in Jesus' steps we go
To seek thy face above.

3 Our residue of days or hours,
Thine, wholly thine, shall be;
And all our consecrated powers
A sacrifice to thee;
Till Jesus in the clouds appear
To saints on earth forgiven,
And bring the grand sabbatic year,
The jubilee of heaven.

299   S. M.   (824)

Watch-night.

THOU Judge of quick and dead,
Before whose bar severe,
With holy joy, or guilty dread,
We all shall soon appear,

2 Our cautioned souls prepare
For that tremendous day,
And fill us now with watchful care,
And stir us up to pray.

3 O may we thus be found,
Obedient to his word;
Attentive to the trumpet's sound,
And looking for our Lord!

4 O may we thus insure
A lot among the blest;
And watch a moment to secure
An everlasting rest!

300   C. M.   (828)

Renewing the covenant.

COME, let us use the grace divine,
    And all, with one accord,
In a perpetual covenant join
    Ourselves to Christ the Lord:

2 Give up ourselves, through Jesus' power,
    His name to glorify;
And promise, in this sacred hour,
    For God to live and die.

3 The covenant we this moment make,
    Be ever kept in mind:
We will no more our God forsake,
    Or cast his words behind.

4 We never will throw off his fear,
    Who hears our solemn vow;
And if thou art well pleased to hear,
    Come down, and meet us now!

5 Thee, Father, Son, and Holy Ghost,
    Let all our hearts receive;
Present with the celestial host,
    The peaceful answer give.

6 To each the covenant blood apply,
    Which takes our sins away;
And register our names on high,
    And keep us to that day.

301   C. M.   (821)

End of the year.

AND now, my soul, another year
    Of thy short life is past;
I cannot long continue here,
    And this may be my last.

2 Awake, my soul! with utmost care
    Thy true condition learn: .

What are thy hopes? how sure? how fair?
What is thy great concern?

3 Behold, another year begins!
Set out afresh for heaven;
Seek pardon for thy former sins,
In Christ so freely given.

4 Devoutly yield thyself to God,
And on his grace depend;
With zeal pursue the heavenly road,
Nor doubt a happy end.

6. NATIONAL SOLEMNITIES.

302   L. M.   (830)
Public fast. Ezek. ix. 4–6.

O RIGHTEOUS God, thou Judge supreme,
We tremble at thy dreadful name!
And all our crying guilt we own,
In dust and tears, before thy throne.

2 Justly might this polluted land
Prove all the vengeance of thy hand;
And, bathed in heaven, thy sword might come,
To drink our blood, and seal our doom.

3 Yet hast thou not a remnant here,
Whose souls are filled with pious fear?
O bring thy wonted mercy nigh,
While prostrate at thy feet they lie!

4 Behold their tears, attend their moan,
Nor turn away their secret groan:
With these we join our humble prayer,
Our nation shield, our country spare.

303   S. M.   (855)
General thanksgiving.

THROUGH all the lofty sky,
Through all th' inferior ground,

7

Th' Almighty Maker shines confessed,
And pours his blessings round.

2 Each year the teeming earth
With flowers and fruits is crowned;
And grass, and herbs, and harvests, grow,
And send their joys around.

3 The world of waters yields
A rich supply of food,
And distant lands their treasures send
Upon the rolling flood.

4 To serve and bless our land
The elements conspire;
And mercies mix themselves with earth,
With ocean, air, and fire.

5 O that the sons of men
To God their songs would raise,
And celebrate his power and love
In never-ceasing praise!

304   L. M.   (856)
General thanksgiving.

WE thank thee, Lord of heaven and earth,
Who hast preserved us from our birth;
Redeemed us oft from death and dread,
And with thy gifts our table spread.

2 We thank thee for thy still small voice,
Which oft has checked our wayward choice;
For life preserved, for senses clear,
And for our friendships, doubly dear.

3 Thy providence has been our stay,
When other helps were far away;
Our constant guide through every stage,
From infancy to riper age.

4 How shall we half our task fulfill?
We thank thee for thy mind and will,
For present joys, for blessings past,
And for the hope of heaven at last.

7. ON A VOYAGE.

305   7s.   (857)

Psalm cvii. 23-32.

LORD, whom winds and seas obey,
Guide us through the watery way;
In the hollow of thy hand
Hide, and bring us safe to land.

2 Jesus, let our faithful mind
Rest, on thee alone reclined;
Every anxious thought repress,
Keep our souls in perfect peace.

3 Keep the souls whom now we leave;
Bid them to each other cleave;
Bid them walk on life's rough rea;
Bid them come by faith to thee.

4 Save, till all these tempests end,
All who on thy love depend:
Waft our happy spirits o'er;
Land us on the heavenly shore.

PART II

FOR SOCIAL WORSHIP.

SECTION I.

Communion of Saints.

306   S. M.   (869)

Opening the exercises.

JESUS, we look to thee,
  Thy promised presence claim;
Thou in the midst of us shalt be,
  Assembled in thy name:
Thy name salvation is,
  Which here we come to prove;
Thy name is life, and health, and peace,
  And everlasting love.

2 Not in the name of pride
  Or selfishness we meet;
From nature's paths we turn aside,
  And worldly thoughts forget:
We meet the grace to take
  Which thou hast freely given;
We meet on earth for thy dear sake,
  That we may meet in heaven.

3 Present we know thou art;
  But O thyself reveal!
Now, Lord, let every bounding heart
  The mighty comfort feel!
O may thy quickening voice
  The death of sin remove,
And bid our inmost souls rejoice
  In hope of perfect love!

307   C. M.   (872)

Opening the exercises.

ALL praise to our redeeming Lord,
  Who joins us by his grace,
And bids us, each to each restored,
  Together seek his face.

2 He bids us build each other up;
  And, gathered into one,
To our high calling's glorious hope
  We hand in hand go on.

3 The gift which he on one bestows,
  We all delight to prove;
The grace through every vessel flows,
  In purest streams of love.

4 And if our fellowship below
  In Jesus be so sweet,
What heights of rapture shall we know
  When round his throne we meet!

308   C. M.   (886)

Joining the Church.—The vow.

WITNESS, ye men and angels, now,
  Before the Lord we speak;
To him we make our solemn vow,
  A vow we dare not break—

2 That long as life itself shall last,
  Ourselves to Christ we yield;
Nor from his cause will we depart,
  Or ever quit the field.

3 We trust not in our native strength,
  But on his grace rely,
That with returning wants, the Lord
  Will all our need supply.

4 O guide our doubtful feet aright,
And keep us in thy ways;
And while we turn our vows to prayers,
Turn thou our prayers to praise!

309   C. M.   (893)

United in Christ.

JESUS, united by thy grace,
And each to each endeared,
With confidence we seek thy face,
And know our prayer is heard.

2 Still let us own our common Lord,
And bear thine easy yoke;
A band of love, a threefold cord,
Which never can be broke.

3 Touched by the loadstone of thy love,
Let all our hearts agree ;
And ever toward each other move,
And ever move toward thee.

4 To thee inseparably joined,
Let all our spirits cleave:
O may we all the loving mind
That was in thee receive!

5 Grant this, and then from all below
Insensibly remove:
Our souls the change shall scarcely know
Made perfect first in love!

310   C. M.   (888)

"Ye are come unto Mount Sion."

HAPPY the souls to Jesus joined,
And saved by grace alone:
Walking in all his ways, they find
Their heaven on earth begun.

2 The Church triumphant in thy love,
Their mighty joys we know:
They sing the Lamb in hymns above,
And we in hymns below.

3 Thee, in thy glorious realm, they praise,
And bow before thy throne;
We, in the kingdom of thy grace—
The kingdoms are but one.

4 The holy to the holiest leads:
From thence our spirits rise;
And he that in thy statutes treads,
Shall meet thee in the skies.

311   C. M.   (892)

Safety in union.

JESUS, great Shepherd of the sheep,
To thee for help we fly:
Thy little flock in safety keep!
For O, the wolf is nigh!

2 He comes, of hellish malice full,
To scatter, tear, and slay;
He seizes every straggling soul
As his own lawful prey.

3 Us into thy protection take,
And gather with thy arm:
Unless the fold we first forsake,
The wolf can never harm.

4 We laugh to scorn his cruel power,
While by our Shepherd's side:
The sheep he never can devour,
Unless he first divide.

5 Together let us sweetly live,
Together let us die;
And each a starry crown receive,
And reign above the sky.

312   S. M.   (887)

Psalm cxxxvii. 5, 6.

I LOVE thy kingdom, Lord,
  The house of thine abode,
The Church our blest Redeemer bought
With his own precious blood.

2 I love thy Church, O God!
  Her walls before thee stand,
Dear as the apple of thine eye, .
  And graven on thy hand.

3 For her my tears shall fall,
  For her my prayers ascend;
To her my cares and toils be given,
  Till toils and cares shall end.

4 Beyond my highest joy
  I prize her heavenly ways,
Her sweet communion, solemn vows,
  Her hymns of love and praise.

313   L. M.   (1011)

Eucharistic vow.

O HAPPY day that fixed my choice
  On thee, my Saviour and my God!
Well may this glowing heart rejoice,
And tell its raptures all abroad.

2 O happy bond that seals my vows
  To him who merits all my love!
Let cheerful anthems fill his house,
While to that sacred shrine I move.

3 'T is done: the great transaction's done!
  I am my Lord's, and he is mine;
He drew me, and I followed on,
Charmed to confess the voice divine.

4 High Heaven that heard the solemn vow,
That vow renewed shall daily hear,
Till in life's latest hour I bow,
And bless in death a bond so dear.

314   7s.   (877, 878)

Love-feast.

COME, and let us sweetly join,
Christ to praise in hymns divine!
Give we all with one accord
Glory to our common Lord;
Hands, and hearts, and voices, raise;
Sing as in the ancient days;
Antedate the joys above;
Celebrate the feast of love.

2 Strive we, in affection strive:
Let the purer flame revive,
Such as in the martyrs glowed,
Dying champions for their God.
We for Christ, our Master, stand,
Lights in a benighted land;
We our dying Lord confess,
We are Jesus' witnesses.

3 Jesus, we thy promise claim:
We are met in thy great name:
In the midst do thou appear,
Manifest thy presence here!
Sanctify us, Lord, and bless!
Breathe thy Spirit, give thy peace;
Thou thyself within us move:
Make our feast a feast of love.

315   S. M.   (908)

Closing the exercises.

BLEST be the tie that binds
Our hearts in Christian love:

The fellowship of kindred minds
Is like to that above.

2 Before our Father's throne
We pour our ardent prayers;
Our fears, our hopes, our aims, are one—
Our comforts and our cares.

3 We share our mutual woes,
Our mutual burdens bear;
And often for each other flows
The sympathizing tear.

4 When we asunder part,
It gives us inward pain;
But we shall still be joined in heart,
And hope to meet again.

5 This glorious hope revives
Our courage by the way;
While each in expectation lives,
And longs to see the day.

6 From sorrow, toil, and pain,
And sin, we shall be free;
And perfect love and friendship reign
Through all eternity.

316   C. M.   (1014)
Gratitude.

WHEN all thy mercies, O my God,
My rising soul surveys,
Transported with the view, I 'm lost
In wonder, love, and praise!

2 O how can words with equal warmth
The gratitude declare
That glows within my ravished heart?
But thou canst read it there!

3 Ten thousand thousand precious gifts
My daily thanks employ;

Nor is the least a cheerful heart,
That tastes those gifts with joy.

4 Through every period of my life
Thy goodness I'll pursue;
And after death, in distant worlds,
The pleasing theme renew.

5 When nature fails, and day and night
Divide thy works no more,
My ever grateful heart, O Lord,
Thy mercies shall adore.

6 Through all eternity to thee
A grateful song I'll raise;
But O, eternity's too short
To utter all thy praise!

317   C. M.   (904)
Mutual aid.

TRY us, O God, and search the ground
Of every sinful heart:
Whate'er of sin in us is found,
O bid it all depart!

2 When to the right or left we stray,
Leave us not comfortless;
But guide our feet into the way
Of everlasting peace.

3 Help us to help each other, Lord,
Each other's cross to bear:
Let each his friendly aid afford,
And feel his brother's care.

4 Help us to build each other up,
Our little stock improve:
. Increase our faith, confirm our hope,
And perfect us in love.

5 Up into thee, our living Head,
Let us in all things grow;

Till thou hast made us free indeed,
And spotless here below.

6 Then, when the mighty work is wrought,
Receive thy ready bride:
Give us in heaven a happy lot
With all the sanctified.

318   C. M.   (910)

Closing the exercises.

GOD of all consolation, take
The glory of thy grace!
Thy gifts to thee we render back
In ceaseless songs of praise.

2 Through thee we now together came,
In singleness of heart:
We met, O Jesus, in thy name,
And in thy name we part.

3 We part in body, not in mind;
Our minds continue one;
And each to each in Jesus joined,
We hand in hand go on.

4 Subsists as in us all one soul;
No power can make us twain;
And mountains rise, and oceans roll,
To sever us in vain.

5 Then let us lawfully contend,
And fight our passage through—
Bear in our faithful minds the end,
And keep the prize in view.

SECTION II.
· Prayer.

319 L. M. (914)

Opening the exercises.

WHAT various hind'rances we meet
In coming to a mercy-seat!
Yet who that knows the worth of prayer
But wishes to be often there?

2 Prayer makes the darkened cloud withdraw;
Prayer climbs the ladder Jacob saw;
Gives exercise to faith and love;
Brings every blessing from above.

3 Restraining prayer, we cease to fight;
Prayer makes the Christian's armor bright;
And Satan trembles when he sees
The weakest saint upon his knees.

4 Have you no words? Ah! think again:
Words flow apace when you complain,
And fill your fellow-creature's ear
With the sad tale of all your care.

5 Were half the breath thus vainly spent,
To Heaven in supplication sent,   *
Your cheerful song would oftener be,
"Hear what the Lord has done for me."

320 L. M. (237 Z.)

The mercy-seat.

FROM every stormy wind that blows,
From every swelling tide of woes,
There is a calm, a sure retreat:
'T is found beneath the mercy-seat.

2 There is a place where Jesus sheds
The oil of gladness on our heads—
A place than all besides more sweet:
It is the blood-bought mercy-seat.

3 There is a scene where spirits blend,
Where friend holds fellowship with friend;
Though sundered far by faith they meet
Around one common mercy-seat.

4 There, there on eagle-wing we soar,
And sin and sense seem all no more;
And heaven comes down our souls to greet,
And glory crowns the mercy-seat.

321   S. M.   (936)

"The violent take it by force."

O MAY thy powerful word
   Inspire a feeble worm
To rush into thy kingdom, Lord,
   And take it as by storm!

2 O may we all improve
   The grace already given,
To seize the crown of perfect love,
   And scale the mount of heaven! .

322   C. M.   (911)

Opening the exercises.

SHEPHERD Divine, our wants relieve,
   In this our evil day:
To all thy tempted followers give
   The power to watch and pray.

2 Long as our fiery trials last,
   Long as the cross we bear,
O let our souls on thee be cast
   In never-ceasing prayer!

3 Till thou thy perfect love impart,
   Till thou thyself bestow,

Be this the cry of every heart—
I will not let thee go—

4 I will not let thee go unless
Thou tell thy name to me,
With all thy great salvation bless,
And make me all like thee.

5 Then let me, on the mountain-top,
Behold thy open face;
Where faith in sight is swallowed up,
And prayer in endless praise.

323　　　　　S. M.　　　　　(912)

Opening the exercises.

THE praying Spirit breathe,
The watching power impart;
From all entanglements beneath
Call off my anxious heart:

2 My feeble mind sustain,
By worldly thoughts oppressed;
Appear, and bid me turn again
To my eternal rest.

3 Swift to my rescue come,
Thine own this moment seize;
Gather my wandering spirit home,
And keep in perfect peace:

4 Suffered no more to rove
O'er all the earth abroad,
Arrest the prisoner of thy love,
And shut me up in God.

324　　　　　C. M.　　　　　(917)

What is prayer?

PRAYER is the soul's sincere desire,
Uttered or unexpressed;

The motion of a hidden fire
That trembles in the breast.

2 Prayer is the burden of a sigh,
The falling of a tear,
The upward glancing of an eye,
When none but God is near.

3 Prayer is the simplest form of speech
That infant lips can try;
Prayer, the sublimest strains that reach
The Majesty on high.

. 4 Prayer is the Christian's vital breath,
The Christian's native air;
His watch-word at the gates of death;
He enters heaven with prayer.

5 Prayer is the contrite sinner's voice,
Returning from his ways,
While angels in their songs rejoice,
And cry, "Behold, he prays!"

6 O thou, by whom we come to God,
The Life, the Truth, the Way!
The path of prayer thyself hast trod:
Lord, teach us how to pray.

325   C. M.   (923)

For the water of life.

FOUNTAIN of life to all below
 Let thy salvation roll;
Water, replenish, and o'erflow,
 Every believing soul.

2 Turn back our nature's rapid tide,
 And we shall flow to thee,
While down the stream of time we glide
 To our eternity.

3 The well of life to us thou art,
Of joy the swelling flood;
Wafted by thee, with willing heart
We swift return to God.

4 We soon shall reach the boundless sea,
Into thy fullness fall;
Be lost and swallowed up in thee,
Our God, our all in all.

326   S. M.   (921)

Wants.

JESUS, my strength, my hope,
On thee I cast my care,
With humble confidence look up,
And know thou hear'st my prayer.
Give me on thee to wait,
Till I can all things do,
On thee, almighty to create,
Almighty to renew.

2 I want a sober mind,
A self-renouncing will,
That tramples down and casts behind
The baits of pleasing ill;
A soul inured to pain,
To hardship, grief, and loss,
Bold to take up, firm to sustain,
The consecrated cross.

3 I want a godly fear,
A quick-discerning eye,
That looks to thee when sin is near,
And sees the tempter fly;
A spirit still prepared,
And armed with jealous care,
Forever standing on its guard,
And watching unto prayer.

327   C. M.   (949)

The benediction.   Num. vi. 24–26.

COME, Father, Son, and Holy Ghost,
  One God in persons three,
Bring back the heavenly blessing lost,
  By all mankind and me.
Thy favor, and thy nature too,
  To me, to all restore:
Forgive, and after God renew,
  And keep us evermore.

2 Eternal Sun of righteousness,
  Display thy beams divine,
And cause the glories of thy face
  Upon my heart to shine.
Light, in thy light, O may I see,
  Thy grace and mercy prove!
Revived, and cheered, and blessed by thee,
  The God of pardoning love.

3 Lift up thy countenance serene,
  And let thy happy child
Behold, without a cloud between,
  The Godhead reconciled.
That all-comprising peace bestow
  On me, through grace forgiven:
The joys of holiness below,
  And then the joys of heaven!

PART III

For Domestic Worship.

The Family.

328   S. M.   (994)

Psalm cxxxiii.

BLEST are the sons of peace,
  Whose hearts and hopes are one;
Whose kind designs to serve and please
  Through all their actions run.

2 Blest is the pious house
  Where zeal and friendship meet;
Their songs of praise, their mingled vows,
  Make their communion sweet.

3 Thus on the heavenly hills
  The saints are blest above,
Where joy, like morning dew, distils,
  And all the air is love.

329   C. M.   (958)

Sabbath morning.   Psalm v. 1-8.

LORD, in the morning thou shalt hear
  My voice ascending high;
To thee will I direct my prayer,
  To thee lift up mine eye:

2 Up to the hills where Christ is gone,
  To plead for all his saints,
Presenting at his Father's throne
  Our songs and our complaints.

3 Thou art a God before whose sight
  The wicked shall not stand;

Sinners shall ne'er be thy delight,
Nor dwell at thy right-hand.
4 But to thy house will I resort,
To taste thy mercies there;
I will frequent thy holy court,
And worship in thy fear.
5 O may thy Spirit guide my feet
In ways of righteousness;
Make every path of duty straight
And plain before my face.

330   L. M.   (951)
Morning.

A WAKE, my soul, and with the sun
Thy daily stage of duty run;
Shake off dull sloth, and early rise
To pay thy morning sacrifice.

2 Wake and lift up thyself, my heart,
And with the angels bear thy part;
Who all night long unwearied sing
High praise to the eternal King.

3 Glory to thee, who safe hast kept,
And hast refreshed me while I slept:
Grant, Lord, when I from death shall wake,
I may of endless life partake.

4 Direct, control, suggest this day,
All I design, or do, or say,
That all my powers, with all their might,
In thy sole glory may unite.

331   L. M.   (959)
Evening.

A LL praise to thee, my God, this night,
For all the blessings of the light:
Keep me, O keep me, King of kings,
Under thine own almighty wings.

2 Forgive me, Lord, for thy dear Son,
The ills that I this day have done;
That with the world, myself, and thee,
I, ere I sleep, at peace may be.

3 Teach me to live that I may dread
The grave as little as my bed;
Teach me to die, that so I may
Rise glorious at the awful day.

4 O may my soul on thee repose,
And with sweet sleep mine eyelids close—
Sleep that may me more vigorous make,
To serve my God, when I awake.

332   7s.   (960)

Evening.

OMNIPRESENT God! whose aid
    No one ever asked in vain,
Be this night about my bed,
    Every evil thought restrain:
Lay thy hand upon my soul,
    God of my unguarded hours!
All my enemies control,
    Hell, and earth, and nature's powers.

2 O thou jealous God! come down,
    God of spotless purity;
Claim and seize me for thine own,
    Consecrate my heart to thee:
Under thy protection take;
    Songs in the night season give;
Let me sleep to thee, and wake;
    Let me die to thee, and live.

333   S. M.   (955)

Morning.

SEE how the morning sun
    Pursues his shining way,

And wide proclaims his Maker's praise,
With every brightening ray.

2 Thus would my rising soul
Its heavenly Parent sing;
And to its great Original
The humble tribute bring.

3 Serene I laid me down,
Beneath his guardian care;
I slept, and I awoke, and found
My kind Preserver near!

4 My life I would anew
Devote, O Lord, to thee;
And in thy service I would spend
A long eternity.

334   S. M.   (963)
Evening.

THE day is past and gone,
The evening shades appear:
O may we all remember well,
The night of death draws near!

2 We lay our garments by,
Upon our beds to rest;
So death will soon disrobe us all
Of what is here possessed.

3 Lord, keep us safe this night,
Secure from all our fears;
May angels guard us, while we sleep,
Till morning light appears.

4 And when we early rise,
And view the unwearied sun,
May we set out to win the prize,
And after glory run.

5 And when our days are past,
And we from time remove,
. O may we in thy bosom rest,
The bosom of thy love!

335   L. M.   (964)

Evening.

THUS far the Lord hath led me on,
    Thus far his power prolongs my days,
And every evening shall make known
    Some fresh memorial of his grace.

2 Much of my time has run to waste,
    And I perhaps am near my home;
But he forgives my follies past,
    And gives me strength for days to come.

3 I lay my body down to sleep,
    Peace is the pillow for my head;
While well-appointed angels keep
    Their watchful stations round my bed.

4 Thus when the night of death shall come,
    My flesh shall rest beneath the ground,
And wait thy voice to rouse my tomb,
    With sweet salvation in the sound.

336   L. M.   (973)

Morning or evening.

MY God, how endless is thy love!
    Thy gifts are every evening new;
And morning mercies from above
    Gently distil like early dew.

2 Thou spread'st the curtains of the night,
    Great Guardian of my sleeping hours;
Thy sovereign word restores the light,
    And quickens all my drowsy powers.

3 I yield myself to thy command;
   To thee devote my nights and days:
Perpetual blessings from thy hand .
   Demand perpetual songs of praise.

337   C. M.   (953)

Morning.

ONCE more, my soul, the rising day
   Salutes thy waking eyes; .
Once more, my voice, thy tribute pay
   To Him that rules thé skies.

2 Night unto night his name repeats,
   The day renews the sound—
Wide as the heavens on which he sits,
   To turn the seasons round.

3 'T is he supports my mortal frame;
   My tongue shall speak his praise:
My sins might rouse his wrath to flame,
   But yet his wrath delays.

4 O God, let all my hours be thine,
   While I enjoy the light!
Then shall my sun in smiles decline,
   And bring a pleasant night.

338   C. M.   (371 Z.)

Child's morning hymn.

THE morning bright, With rosy light,
   Has waked me up from sleep:
Father, I own Thy love alone
   Thy little one doth keep.

2 All through the day, I humbly pray,
   Be thou my guard and guide:
My sins forgive, And let me live,
   Blest Jesus, near thy side.

3 O make thy rest Within my breast,
  Great Spirit of all grace:
Make me like thee, Then shall I be
  Prepared to see thy face.

339　　　　C. M.　　　(372 Z.)

Child's evening hymn.

THE daylight fades: The evening shades
　Are gathering round my head:
Father above, I praise that love
Which smooths and guards my bed.

2 While thou art near, I need not fear
  The gloom of midnight hour:
Blest Jesus, still From every ill
  Defend me with thy power.

3 Pardon my sin, And enter in
  And sanctify my heart:
Spirit divine, O make me thine,
  And ne'er from me depart!

340　　　　C. M.　　　(969)

Evening.

DREAD Sovereign, let my evening song
　Like holy incense rise;
Assist the offerings of my tongue
  To reach the lofty skies.

2 Through all the dangers of the day
  Thy hand was still my guard;
And still to drive my wants away
  Thy mercy stood prepared.

3 Sprinkled afresh with pardoning blood,
  I lay me down to rest;
As in the embraces of my God,
  Or on my Saviour's breast.

341　　　　8,7.　.　　(961)

Evening.

SAVIOUR, breathe an evening blessing
Ere repose our spirits seal:
Sin and want we come confessing;
　Thou canst save and thou canst heal.

2 Though destruction walk around us,
　Though the arrow past us fly,
Angel-guards from thee surround us;
　We are safe, if thou art nigh.

3 Though the night be dark and dreary,
　Darkness cannot hide from thee;
Thou art he who, never weary,
　Watcheth where thy people be.

4 Should swift death this night o'ertake us,
　And our couch become our tomb,
May the morn in heaven awake us,
　Clad in light, and deathless bloom.

342　　　　C. M.　　　(965)

Evening.

NOW from the altar of our hearts
Let warmest thanks arise;
Assist us, Lord, to offer up　　・
　Our evening sacrifice.

2 This day God was our sun and shield,
　Our keeper and our guide;
His care was on our weakness shown,
　His mercies multiplied.

3 Minutes and mercies multiplied,
　Have made up all this day;
Minutes came quick, but mercies were
　More fleet and free than they.

4 New time, new favors, and new joys,
   Do a new song require:
Till we shall praise thee as we would,
   Accept our hearts' desire.

SECTION II.

The Closet.

343   C. M.   (1009)

"My meditation of him shall be sweet."

WHILE thee I seek, protecting Power!
   Be my vain wishes stilled;
And may this consecrated hour
   With better hopes be filled.

2 Thy love the power of thought bestowed,
   To thee my thoughts would soar:
Thy mercy o'er my life has flowed;
   That mercy I adore.

3 In each event of life, how clear
   Thy ruling hand I see!
Each blessing to my soul most dear,
   Because conferred by thee.

4 In every joy that crowns my days,
   In every pain I bear,
My heart shall find delight in praise,
   Or seek relief in prayer.

5 When gladness wings the favored hour,
   Thy love my thoughts shall fill;
Resigned, when storms of sorrow lower,
   My soul shall meet thy will.

6 My lifted eye, without a tear,
  The gathering storm shall see;
My steadfast heart shall know no fear—
  That heart will rest on thee.

344   8,7.   (1046

The departing saint.

HAPPY soul, thy days are ended,
  All thy mourning-days below;
Go, by angel-guards attended,
  To the sight of Jesus, go!
Waiting to receive thy spirit,
  Lo! the Saviour stands above;
Shows the purchase of his merit,
  Reaches out the crown of love.

2 Struggle through thy latest passion,
  To thy great Redeemer's breast—
To his uttermost salvation,
  To his everlasting rest.
For the joy he sets before thee,
  Bear a momentary pain—
Die, to live a life of glory!
  Suffer, with thy Lord to reign.

Benedictions and Doxologies.

345   8,7.   (1050)

Dismission.

LORD, dismiss us with thy blessing,
Bid us now depart in peace;
Still on heavenly manna feeding,
Let our faith and love increase:
Fill each breast with consolation;
Up to thee our hearts we raise:
When we reach our blissful station,
Then we'll give thee nobler praise.

GLORIA PATRI.

346   S. M.   (1052)

GIVE to the Father praise;
Give glory to the Son;
And to the Spirit of his grace
Be equal honor done.

347   C. M.   (1053)

NOW let the Father, and the Son,
And Spirit be adored,
Where there are works to make him known,
Or saints to love the Lord.

348   L. M.   (1054)

PRAISE God, from whom all blessings flow;
Praise him, all creatures here below;
Praise him above, ye heavenly host;
Praise Father, Son, and Holy Ghost.

349   L. M.

PRAISE to the Father, and the Son,
And Holy Spirit—Three in One;
As 't was of old, is now, shall be,
Ascribed to all eternity!

MISCELLANY.

350   8,7.

I will go to Jesus.

LADEN with a heavy burden,
    To my Saviour I will go,
Casting all my care upon him,
    He will bear my load, I know.

Refrain.

I will go, with all my guilt, to Jesus,
    Wretched, poor, and helpless though I be;
I will go and wash my spirit in the fountain—
    His blood shall set me free.

2 Jesus is the burden-bearer;
    All my sins on him were laid;
Dying on the cross accursèd,
    He a full atonement made.

3 At the feet of Jesus falling,
    Rent with anguish, pain, and grief,
Of my crimes with tears repenting,
    He will give me sweet relief.

4 By his grace and mercy pardoned,
    All my sins and guilt forgiven,
I will thank, and bless, and praise him,
    For the joyful hope of heaven.

351   6,4,6,4,6,6,4.   (519 Z.)

Nearer, my God, to thee.

NEARER, my God, to thee,
    Nearer to thee,
E'en though it be a cross
    That raiseth me;
Still all my song shall be,
Nearer, my God, to thee,
    Nearer to thee.

2 Though like the wanderer,
   The sun gone down,
Darkness be over me,
   My rest a stone;
Yet in my dreams I'd be
Nearer, my God, to thee,
   Nearer to thee.

3 There let the way appear
   Steps unto heaven;
All that thou sendest me
   In mercy given;
Angels to beckon me
Nearer, my God, to thee,
   Nearer to thee.

852   6,4,6,4,6,6,4.
       Nearer, my God, to thee.

NEARER, my God, to thee—
   Nearer, I sigh:
Nearer, I fain would be—
   Nearer, still cry!
Nearer, when woes assail,
Nearer, when joys prevail—
   Nearer to thee!

2 The world is dark and drear—
   I feel so lone:
Beset with sin and fear—
   I sigh and moan;
Nor can I comfort see
Till I can nearer be—
   Nearer to thee!

3 The crosses on me laid
   Still press me down:
One cross can give me aid—
   One cross alone—
The cross of Calvary—
My Saviour's cross—lifts me
   Nearer to thee!

353

The precious name.

TAKE the name of Jesus with you,
  Child of sorrow and of woe—
It will joy and comfort give you;
  Take it, then, where'er you go.

Chorus.

Precious name, O how sweet!
  Hope of earth and joy of heaven;
Precious name, O how sweet!
  Hope of earth and joy of heaven.

2 Take the name of Jesus ever,
  As a shield from every snare;
If temptations 'round you gather,
  Breathe that holy name in prayer.

3 O the precious name of Jesus!
  How it thrills our souls with joy,
When his loving arms receive us,
  And his songs our tongues employ!

4 At the name of Jesus bowing,
  Falling prostrate at his feet,
King of kings in heaven we'll crown him,
  When our journey is complete.

354

9s.

Sweet by and by.

THERE'S a land that is fairer than day,
  And by faith we may see it afar,
For the Father waits over the way,
  To prepare us a dwelling-place there.

Chorus.

In the sweet by and by,
We shall meet on that beautiful shore.
  In the sweet by and by,
We shall meet on that beautiful shore.

2 We shall sing on that beautiful shore
   The melodious songs of the blest,
And our spirits shall sorrow no more—
   Not a sigh for the blessing of rest.

3 To our bountiful Father above
   We will offer the tribute of praise,
For the glorious gift of his love,
   And the blessings that hallow our days.

355   7s.

I am coming to the cross.

I AM coming to the cross;
   I am poor, and weak, and blind;
I am counting all but dross,
   I shall full salvation find.

Chorus.—I am trusting, Lord, in thee,
   Blessèd Lamb of Calvary;
   Humbly at thy cross I bow;
   Save me, Jesus, save me now.

2 Long my heart has sighed for thee,
   Long has evil reigned within;
Jesus sweetly speaks to me,
   "I will cleanse you from all sin."

3 Here I give my all to thee,
   Friends, and time, and earthly store;
Soul and body thine to be—
   Wholly thine forevermore.

4 In thy promises I trust,
   Now I feel the blood applied:
I am prostrate in the dust,
   I with Christ am crucified.

5 Jesus comes! he fills my soul!
   Perfected in him I am;
I am every whit made whole:
   Glory, glory to the Lamb!

8

356   10,8.

Gathering home.

UP to the bountiful Giver of life—
  Gathering home! gathering home!
Up to the dwelling where cometh no strife,
The dear ones are gathering home.

Chorus.

Gathering home! gathering home!
  Never to sorrow more, never to roam,
Gathering home! gathering home!
  God's children are gathering home.

2 Up to the city where falleth no night—
  Gathering home! gathering home!
Up where the Saviour's own face is the light,
The dear ones are gathering home.

3 Up to the beautiful mansions above—
  Gathering home! gathering home!
Safe in the arms of his infinite love,
The dear ones are gathering home.

357   8s.

"I go to prepare a place for you."   John xiv. 2.

O THINK of a home over there,
  By the side of the river of light,
Where the saints, all immortal and fair,
Are robed in their garments of white.

Refrain.

Over there, over there,
  O think of a home over there!
Over there, over there,
  O think of a home over there!

2 O think of the friends over there,
  Who before us the journey have trod,
Of the songs that they breathe on the air,
In their home in the palace of God.

3 My Saviour is now over there,
  There my kindred and friends are at rest;
Then away from my sorrow and care,
  Let me fly to the land of the blest.
4 I'll soon be at home over there,
  For the end of my journey I see:
Many dear to my heart over there,
  Are watching and waiting for me.

358   7,5,8.

Joy in heaven.

THERE is joy in heaven to-day!
  There is joy to-day
O'er the lamb that is found again,
Far away from pastures green,
  Wandering all alone,
On the desolate, barren plain.

Refrain.

Glory to the Lord of hosts,
  Shout the morning stars on high,
Praise him ever, ye angels of light!
  He has heard the distant cry
    Of the lamb to-day,
And he bears it rejoicing home.

2 When a soul has gone astray
From the narrow way,
  And there seemeth no joy nor rest,
Jesus still is ever near,
Hearing, night and day,
  All the cries of the sin-oppressed.

3 Sinner, bow with gratitude,
And, with heart subdued,
  Plead his mercy and pardon free.
He will see the falling tear,
Hear the fervent prayer,
  And will tenderly welcome thee.

359   7,9.
Every day and hour.

SAVIOUR! more than life to me,
I am clinging, clinging close to thee;
Let thy precious blood applied,
Keep me ever, ever near thy side.

Refrain.—Every day, every hour,
    Let me feel thy cleansing power;
    May thy tender love to me
    Bind me closer, closer, Lord, to thee.

2 Through this changing world below
Lead me gently, gently as I go;
Trusting thee, I cannot stray—
I can never, never lose my way.

3 Let me love thee more and more,
Till this fleeting, fleeting life is o'er;
Till my soul is lost in love,
In a brighter, brighter world above.

360   8,7.
What a friend we have in Jesus.

WHAT a friend we have in Jesus,
    All our sins and griefs to bear!
What a privilege to carry
    Every thing to God in prayer!
O what peace we often forfeit!
    O what needless pain we bear!
All because we do not carry
    Every thing to God in prayer.

2 Have we trials and temptations?
    Is there trouble anywhere?
We should never be discouraged—
    Take it to the Lord in prayer.
Can we find a Friend so faithful,
    Who will all our sorrows share?

Jesus knows our every weakness—
Take it to the Lord in prayer.

3 Are we weak and heavy-laden,
Cumbered with a load of care?
Precious Saviour! still our refuge—
Take it to the Lord in prayer.
Do thy friends despise, forsake thee?
Take it to the Lord in prayer;
In his arms he'll take and shield thee—
Thou wilt find a solace there.

361   8,9.
Hear Him calling.

ARE you staying, safely staying,
In the tender Shepherd's peaceful fold?
No, I'm straying, sadly straying,
On the lonely mountains, dark and cold.

Refrain.

On your ear his loving tones are falling,
For he seeks you, wheresoe'er you roam;
Hear him calling, sweetly calling,
As he bids his wandering sheep come home

2 Are you hearing, gladly hearing,
How he bids his folded flock rejoice?
No, I'm fearing, sadly fearing—
I have followed far the stranger's voice.

3 Are you roaming, longer roaming,
In the cold, dark night of doubt and sin?
No, I'm coming, quickly coming!
Open, Door, make haste to let me in!

362   7,8.
Jesus will forgive.

COME, ye sinners, come to-day,
Jesus will forgive you freely;

All your sins he'll wash away,
Jesus will forgive you freely.

Refrain.—O come to-day!
Why longer stay away?
He will not say you nay;
Jesus will forgive you freely.

2 Come unto the mercy-seat,
Jesus will forgive you freely;
Humbly falling at his feet,
Jesus will forgive you freely.

3 Lay your treasures up above,
Jesus will forgive you freely;
Trust the riches of his love,
Jesus will forgive you freely.

4 Earnestly a blessing seek,
Jesus will forgive you freely;
Trembling sinner, faint and weak,
Jesus will forgive you freely.

5 He is able all to save,
Jesus will forgive you freely;
For your love his blood he gave,
Jesus will forgive you freely.

6 Then, ye sinners, come to-day,
Jesus will forgive you freely;
All your sins he'll wash away,
Jesus will forgive you freely.

363   7,6.   (457 Z.)

O when shall I see Jesus?

O WHEN shall I see Jesus,
And reign with him above,
And drink the flowing fountain
Of everlasting love?

When shall I be delivered
From this vain world of sin,
And with my blessèd Jesus
Drink endless pleasures in?

Refrain.—Christ is all the world to me,
And his glory I shall see;
And before I'd leave my Saviour,
I'd lay me down and die.

2 But now I am a soldier;
My Captain's gone before,
He's given me my orders,
And bids me not give o'er;
And, if I hold out-faithful,
A crown of life he'll give;
And all his valiant soldiers
Shall ever with him live.

3 Whenc'er you meet with troubles
And trials on your way,
O cast your care on Jesus,
And don't forget to pray!
Gird on the heavenly armor
Of faith, and hope, and love;
And when the combat's ended,
You'll reign with him above.

364 L. M.
By and by.

IT may be far, it may be near;
There is a hope, there is a fear;
But in the future waiting, I
Shall Jesus see, yes, "by and by."

Chorus.—By and by, yes, by and by,
By and by, yes, by and by;
But in the future waiting, I
Shall Jesus see, yes, "by and by."

2 Impatient soul, and murmuring heart,
Your murmuring cease, and bear your part
Of pain and labor on life's road,
For soon 't will lead thee to thy God.

3 Yes, "by and by" will soon be now,
And God shall wipe each tear-stained brow;
The Lamb shall feed them from the throne,
To living fountains lead his own.

4 O verdant fields! O shining shore!
The Lamb of God spreads wide the door;
Ah, golden city, surely I
Shall see thy glories "by and by!"

365　　　　　'8,7.　　　　(304 Z.)
Gone to heaven.

WHY lament the Christian dying?
　　Why indulge in tears or gloom?
Calmly on the Lord relying,
　　He can greet the opening tomb.

Refrain.—We'll meet again, by and by!
　　　　We'll meet again, by and by!
　　　In the realms of endless glory
　　　　We shall meet, yes, by and by.

2 Scenes seraphic, high, and glorious,
　　Now forbid his longer stay;
See him rise, o'er death victorious!
　　Angels beckon him away.

3 Hark, the golden harps are ringing!
　　Sounds unearthly fill his ear:
Millions now in heaven singing,
　　Greet his joyful entrance there.

366　　　　　L. M.
He leadeth me.

HE leadeth me! O blessèd thought!
　O words with heavenly comfort fraught!

Whate'er I do, where'er I be,
Still 't is God's hand that leadeth me!

Chorus.—He leadeth me, leadeth me;
He leadeth me,
By his own hand he leadeth me.

2 Sometimes, 'mid scenes of deepest gloom,
Sometimes, where Eden's bowers bloom,
By waters still, o'er troubled sea—
Still 't is his hand that leadeth me!

3 Lord, I would clasp thy hand in mine,
Nor ever murmur nor repine:
Content, whatever lot I see,
Since 't is my God that leadeth me!

4 And when my task on earth is done,
When, by thy grace, the victory's won,
E'en death's cold wave I will not flee,
Since God through Jordan leadeth me!

367   8s.

The Rock that is higher than I.

O SOMETIMES the shadows are deep,
And rough seems the path to the goal,
And sorrows, sometimes how they sweep
Like tempests down over the soul!

Chorus.

O then to the Rock let me fly,
To the Rock that is higher than I!
O then to the Rock let me fly,
To the Rock that is higher than I!

2 O sometimes how long seems the day,
And sometimes how weary my feet!
But toiling in life's dusty way,
The Rock's blessèd shadow how sweet!

3 O near to the Rock let me keep,
If blessings or sorrows prevail;

Or climbing the mountain-way steep,
Or walking the shadowy vale!
  Then, quick to the Rock I can fly,
  To the Rock that is higher than I.

368   9,4.
Footsteps of Jesus.

SWEETLY, Lord, have we heard thee calling,
  Come, follow me!
And we see where thy foot-prints falling,
  Lead us to thee.

Chorus.

Foot-prints of Jesus, that make the pathway
    glow;
We will follow the steps of Jesus where'er
  . they go.

2 Though they lead o'er the cold, dark mount-
      ains,
  Seeking his sheep;
Or along by Siloam's fountains,
  Helping the weak.

3 If they lead through the temple holy,
  Preaching the word;
Or in homes of the poor and lowly,
  Serving the Lord.

4 Though, dear Lord, in thy pathway keeping,
  We follow thee;
Through the gloom of that place of weeping,
  Gethsemane!

5 If thy way and its sorrows bearing,
  We go again,
Up the slope of the hill-side, bearing
  Our cross of pain.

6 By and by, through the shining portals,
  Turning our feet,

We shall walk with the glad immortals
Heaven's golden street.

7 Then at last, when on high he sees us,
Our journey done,
We will rest where the steps of Jesus
End at his throne.

369   11s.

Revive us again.

ALL glory and praise be to Jesus our Lord,
So plenteous in grace, and so true to his
word.

Refrain.—Hallelujah! thine the glory,
Hallelujah! Amen.
Hallelujah! thine the glory,
Revive us again.

2 To us he hath given the gift from above—
The earnest of heaven, the Spirit of love.

3 Ye all may receive, who on Jesus do call,
The gift of his Spirit—'t is proffered to all.

4 The peace and the power ye sinners embrace,
And look for the shower—the Spirit of grace.

INDEX OF HYMNS.

* Attributed to C. Wesley, first printed 1757.
† Generally attributed to R. Robinson, but more recently to Lady Huntingdon.

---

* Imitation of an old Latin hymn: it has been erroneously attributed to J. Montgomery, Burkitt, David Dickson, and others, who
printed it, with variations, from an old MS. in the British Museum.

---

* From a Collection of Psalms and Hymns, by J. and W. Oliver, London, 1774.

* From "Pocket Hymn-book," the first Hymn-book published for the Methodist Episcopal Church, by Bishops Coke and Asbury—attributed to Olivers. 1769.
† From a translation of a Latin hymn by St. Bernard, by Anthony William Boehm, abridged in "A Collection of Psalms and Hymns," by J. and C. Wesley, 1741.

*Attributed by some to Christopher Batty: it has also been credited to several others—particularly James Allen and W. Shirley.

INDEX TO MISCELLANY.

The Discipline of the M. E. Church, South, contains this Directory:

Ques. 1. What directions are given for uniformity in public worship?

Ans. 1. The morning service shall be conducted in the following order:

(1) Singing—the congregation standing.

(2) Prayer—the congregation kneeling.

(3) Reading a lesson out of the Old Testament and another out of the New.

(4) Singing—the congregation sitting.

(5) Preaching.

(6) Singing—the congregation standing.

(7) Prayer—the congregation kneeling.

(8) Benediction.

2. The afternoon and evening service shall be the same as the morning, except that one of the lessons, or both, may be omitted, at the discretion of the minister.

3. The Lord's Supper shall be administered monthly, in every congregation, wherever it is practicable; and where it is not, at every quarterly meeting. Let the service preceding the administration be so proportioned as to admit of due time for this solemn ordinance.

4. Let the Lord's Prayer be used on all occasions of public worship, in concluding the first morning prayer, the congregation repeating after the minister; and the apostolic benediction (2 Cor. xiii. 14) in dismissing the congregation.

5. The Ritual shall be invariably used in all the offices for which it is prescribed.

USE OF THE RITUAL.

And let all the people say,
Amen.

This is a very ancient and scriptural part of the liturgy.

When the baptism of infants or adults is performed, let every one present turn to the Ritual for the occasion, and at the end of each petition by the minister (as laid down) say, audibly, *Amen.*

So, also, in the administration of the Lord's Supper.

The congregation are thus joined together in the solemn service, and are not spectators, but worshipers.

When the vows are taken, as in adult baptism and the reception or recognition of Churchmembers, the candidates in each case should be supplied with the book, and answer accordingly.

THE MINISTRATION OF BAPTISM TO INFANTS.

The minister, coming to the font, which is to be filled with pure water, shall use the following, or some other suitable exhortation:

, Dearly beloved, forasmuch as all men are conceived and born in sin, and that our Saviour Christ saith, Except a man be born of water and of the Spirit, he cannot enter into the kingdom of God: I beseech you to call upon God the Father, through our Lord Jesus Christ, that of his bounteous mercy he will grant to *this child* that which by nature *he* cannot have: that *he* may be baptized with water and the Holy Ghost, and received into Christ's holy

Church, and be made *a lively member* of the same.

Then shall the minister say,
Let us pray.

Almighty and everlasting God, we beseech thee for thine infinite mercies, that thou wilt look upon *this child:* wash *him* and sanctify *him* with the Holy Ghost; that *he,* being delivered from thy wrath, may be received into the ark of Christ's Church, and being steadfast in faith, joyful through hope, and rooted in love, may so pass the waves of this troublesome world, that finally *he* may come to the land of everlasting life, there to reign with thee, world without end, through Jesus Christ our Lord. *Amen.*

O merciful God, grant that the old Adam in *this child* may be so buried, that the new man may be raised up in *him.* *Amen.*

Grant that all carnal affections may die in *him,* and that all things belonging to the Spirit may live and grow in *him.* *Amen.*

Grant that *he* may have power and strength to have victory, and to triumph against the devil, the world, and the flesh. *Amen.*

Grant that whosoever is dedicated to thee by our office and ministry may also be endued with heavenly virtues, and everlastingly rewarded through thy mercy, O blessed Lord God, who dost live and govern all things, world without end. *Amen.*

Almighty, ever-living God, whose most dearly-beloved Son Jesus Christ, for the forgiveness of our sins, did shed out of his most precious side both water and blood, and gave commandment to his disciples that they should go teach all nations, and baptize them in the name of the Father, and of the Son, and of the Holy

Ghost: regard, we beseech thee, the supplications of thy congregation; and grant that *this child*, now to be baptized, may receive the fullness of thy grace, and ever remain in the number of thy faithful and elect children, through Jesus Christ our Lord. *Amen.*

Then shall the people stand up; and the minister
shall say,
Hear the words of the Gospel, written by St. Mark, in the tenth chapter, at the thirteenth verse: .

They brought young children to Christ, that he should touch them. And his disciples rebuked those that brought them; but when Jesus saw it, he was much displeased, and said unto them, Suffer the little children to come unto me, and forbid them not, for of such is the kingdom of God. Verily I say unto you, Whosoever shall not receive the kingdom of God as a little child, he shall not enter therein. And he took them up in his arms, put his hands upon them, and blessed them.

Then the minister, addressing the parents, or others
presenting the child, shall say,

In causing *this child* to be brought by baptism into the Church of Christ, it is your duty to teach *him* to renounce the devil and all his works, the vain pomp and glory of the world, with all covetous desires of the same, and the carnal desires of the flesh, so that he may not follow or be led by them; to believe all the articles of the Christian faith; and to obediently keep God's holy will and commandments all the days of *his* life.

Then the minister shall take the child into his hands,
if convenient, and say to the friends of the child,

Name this child.

And then, naming it after them, he shall sprinkle or pour water upon it (or, if desired, immerse it in water), saying,

N., I baptize thee in the name of the Father, and of the Son, and of the Holy Ghost. *Amen.*

The minister may, at his discretion, lay hands on the subject, accompanying the act with a suitable invocation, and then, all kneeling, close with extemporaneous devotions and the Lord's Prayer.

Our Father who art in heaven, hallowed be thy name; thy kingdom come; thy will be done on earth, as it is in heaven; give us this day our daily bread; and forgive us our trespasses, as we forgive those who trespass against us; and lead us not into temptation, but deliver us from evil. *Amen.*

THE MINISTRATION OF BAPTISM TO SUCH AS ARE OF RIPER YEARS.

The minister, coming to the font, which is to be filled with pure water, shall use the following, or some other suitable exhortation:

Dearly beloved, forasmuch as all men are conceived and born in sin (and that which is born of the flesh is flesh, and they that are in the flesh cannot please God, but live in sin, committing many actual transgressions), and that our Saviour Christ saith, Except a man be born of water and of the Spirit, he cannot enter into the kingdom of God: I beseech you to call upon God the Father, through our Lord Jesus Christ, that of his bounteous goodness he will grant to *these persons* that which by nature *they* cannot have: that *they* may be baptized with water and the Holy Ghost, and received into Christ's holy Church, and be made lively *members* of the same.

Then shall the minister say,

Almighty and immortal God, the aid of all that need, the helper of all that flee to thee for succor, the life of them that believe, and the resurrection of the dead · we call upon thee for *these persons* now to be baptized. Receive *them*, O Lord, as thou hast promised by thy well-beloved Son, saying, Ask, and ye shall receive; seek, and ye shall find; knock, and it shall be opened unto you: so give now unto us that ask; let us that seek find; open the gate unto us that knock; that *these persons* may enjoy the everlasting benediction of thy heavenly washing, and may come to the eternal kingdom which thou hast promised by Christ our Lord. *Amen.*

Then shall the people stand up, and the minister shall say,

Hear the words of the Gospel, written by St. John, in the third chapter, beginning at the first verse:

There was a man of the Pharisees, named Nicodemus, a ruler of the Jews: the same came to Jesus by night, and said unto him, Rabbi, we know that thou art a teacher come from God; for no man can do these miracles that thou doest, except God be with him. Jesus answered and said unto him, Verily, verily, I say unto thee, Except a man be born again, he cannot see the kingdom of God. Nicodemus saith unto him, How can a man be born when he is old? Can he enter the second time into his mother's womb, and be born? Jesus answered, Verily, verily, I say unto thee, Except

a man be born of water, and of the Spirit, he
cannot enter into the kingdom of God. That
which is born of the flesh is flesh; and that
which is born of the Spirit is spirit. Marvel
not that I said unto thee, Ye must be born
again. The wind bloweth where it listeth, and
thou hearest the sound thereof, but canst not
tell whence it cometh, and whither it goeth;
so is every one that is born of the Spirit.

Then the minister shall speak to the persons to be
baptized on this wise:

Well-beloved, who *are* come hither, desiring
to receive holy baptism, *ye have* heard how the
congregation hath prayed that our Lord Jesus
Christ would vouchsafe to receive *you*, and bless
you, to release *you* of *your* sins, to give *you* the
kingdom of heaven, and everlasting life. And
our Lord Jesus Christ hath promised in his
holy word to grant all those things that we
have prayed for; which promise he for his part
will most surely keep and perform.

Wherefore after this promise made by Christ,
ye must also faithfully, for *your* part, promise,
in the presence of this whole congregation,
that *ye will* renounce the devil and all his works,
and constantly believe God's holy word, and
obediently keep his commandments.

Then shall the minister demand of each of the persons to be baptized, severally:

Ques. Dost thou renounce the devil and all
his works, the vain pomp and glory of the
world, with all covetous desires of the same,
and the carnal desires of the flesh, so that thou
wilt not follow or be led by them?

Ans. I renounce them all.

Ques. Dost thou believe in God the Father
Almighty, maker of heaven and earth? and in

Jesus Christ, his only-begotten Son, our Lord? and that he was conceived by the Holy Ghost, born of the Virgin Mary? that he suffered under Pontius Pilate, was crucified, dead, and buried? that he rose again the third day? that he ascended into heaven, and sitteth at the right-hand of God the Father Almighty, and from thence shall come again, at the end of the world, to judge the quick and the dead?

And dost thou believe in the Holy Ghost, the Church of God, the communion of saints, the remission of sins, the resurrection of the body, and everlasting life after death?

Ans. All this I steadfastly believe.

Ques. Wilt thou be baptized in this faith?

Ans. This is my desire.

Ques. Wilt thou then obediently keep God's holy will and commandments, and walk in the same all the days of thy life?

Ans. I will endeavor so to do, God being my helper.

Then shall the minister say,

O merciful God, grant that the old Adam *in these persons* may be so buried, that the new man may be raised up in *them.* *Amen.*

Grant that all carnal affections may die in *them,* and that all things belonging to the Spirit may live and grow in *them.* *Amen.*

Grant that *they* may have power and strength to have victory, and to triumph against the devil, the world, and the flesh. *Amen.*

Grant that *they,* being here dedicated to thee by our office and ministry, may also be endued with heavenly virtues, and everlastingly re-warded, through thy mercy, O blessed Lord God, who dost live and govern all things, world without end. *Amen.*

Almighty, ever-living God, whose most dear-ly-beloved Son Jesus Christ, for the forgive-ness of our sins, did shed out of his most pre-cious side both water and blood; and gave commandment to his disciples, that they should go teach all nations, and baptize them in the name of the Father, and of the Son, and of the Holy Ghost: regard, we beseech thee, the supplications of this congregation; and grant that the *persons* now to be baptized may receive the fullness of thy grace, and ever remain in the number of thy faithful and elect children, through Jesus Christ our Lord. *Amen.*

Then shall the minister take each person to be bap-tized by the right-hand; and placing him conven-iently by the font, according to his discretion, shall ask the name; and then shall sprinkle or pour water upon him (or, if he shall desire it, shall immerse him in water), saying,

N., I baptize thee in the name of the Father, and of the Son, and of the Holy Ghost. *Amen.*

The minister may, at his discretion, lay hands on the subject, accompanying the act with a suitable invo-cation.

FORM OF THE RECEPTION AND RECOGNI-TION OF CHURCH-MEMBERS.

The minister shall cause the candidates to be placed conveniently before the congregation, and after baptizing any who may not have been previously baptized, he shall say:

Brethren, the Church is of God, and will be preserved to the end of time, for the promotion of his worship and the due administration of his word and ordinances—the maintenance of Christian fellowship and discipline—the edification of believers, and the conversion of the world. All, of every age and station, stand in need of the means of grace which it alone supplies; and it invites all alike to become fellow-citizens with the saints and of the household of God. But as none who have arrived at years of discretion can remain within its pales, or be admitted to its communion, without assuming its obligations, it is my duty to demand of these persons present whether they are resolved to assume the same.

Then shall the minister address the candidates, as follows:

Dearly beloved, you profess to have a desire to flee from the wrath to come, and to be saved from your sins; you seek the fellowship of the people of God, to assist you in working out your salvation; I therefore demand of you:

Do you solemnly, in the presence of God and this congregation, ratify and confirm the promise and vow of repentance, faith, and obedience, contained in the baptismal covenant?

Ans. I do, God being my helper.

Will you be subject to the discipline of the Church, attend upon its ordinances, and support its institutions?

Ans. I will endeavor so to do, by the help of God.

The minister shall then say to the candidates:

We rejoice to recognize you as members of the Church of Christ, and bid you welcome to all its privileges; and in token of our brotherly love, we give you the right-hand of fellowship, and pray that you may be both numbered with his people here, and with his saints in glory everlasting.

The minister shall then say to the congregation:

Brethren, I commend to your love and care these persons whom we this day recognize as members of the Church of Christ. Do all in your power to increase their faith, confirm their hope, and perfect them in love.

Then may follow a hymn suitable to the occasion (as 881–889—New Hymn-book, 308–313), and the minister shall say,

Let us pray.

Almighty God, we thank thee for founding thy Church, and promising that the gates of hell shall not prevail against it. We bless thee for calling us to the fellowship of thy people, and for numbering us with the sons and daughters of the Lord Almighty. We especially praise thy name for enabling these thy servants to avouch the Lord to be their God. Help them to perform the promise and vow which they have made, to renounce the devil, the world, and the flesh; to believe the record which thou hast given of thy Son; and to walk in all thy commandments and ordinances blameless, to the end of their lives. May their communion with thy people be sanctified to their growth in grace and in the knowledge of our Lord and Saviour Jesus Christ, being nourished and knit together, increasing with the increase of God. May thy people do them good, and may they prove a blessing to thy people. And grant, O Lord, that all who are here members of thy militant Church, through thy mercy, the merit of thy Son, and the grace of thy Spirit, may finally be made members of thy triumphant Church in heaven. *Amen.*

Almighty and everlasting God, Heavenly Father, we give thee humble thanks, for that thou hast vouchsafed to call us to the knowledge of thy grace, and faith in thee: increase this knowledge and confirm this faith in us evermore. Give thy Holy Spirit to these persons, that they, being born again, may be made heirs of everlasting salvation, through our Lord Jesus Christ, who liveth and reigneth with thee and the Holy Spirit, now and forever. *Amen.*

Our Father who art in heaven, hallowed be thy name; thy kingdom come; thy will be done on earth, as it is in heaven; give us this day our daily bread; and forgive us our trespasses, as we forgive those who trespass against us; and lead us not into temptation, but deliver us from evil. *Amen.*

THE END.